Nuclear Madness in South Asia

Nuclear Madness in South Asia

Musa Khan Jalalzai

Vij Books India Pvt Ltd

New Delhi (India)

Published by

Vij Books India Pvt Ltd
(Publishers, Distributors & Importers)
2/19, Ansari Road
Delhi – 110 002
Phones: 91-11-43596460, 91-11-47340674
Mobile: 98110 94883
e-mail: contact@vijpublishing.com
www.vijbooks.com

Copyright © 2020, *Author*

ISBN: 978-93-89620-77-1 (Paperback)
ISBN: 978-93-89620-78-8 (ebook)

Contents

Introduction

The tension between the world's two nuclear powers has flared once again in June 2020 along their disputed border-prompting fears of an inadvertent escalation. Ladakh, where clashes took place, belongs to Kashmir-an area that has been challenged since the partition in 1947. In India, (Antara Ghosal Singh - 02 June 2020) "the current crisis at the border has been seen as a continuation of China's post-pandemic "assertive foreign policy" across the world since 2019. Chinese intervention in Ladakh has prompted a military confrontation between the two nuclear states. On 16 June 2020, Chinese army killed 20 Indian soldiers to exhibit its military power of fighting against any challenging state in South Asia. On 19 May, 2020, the EurAsia Times warned that Aksai Chin will be the next flashpoint between India and China, as Chinese newspapers accused the Indian government of constructing military installations in Galwan Valley, a region controlled by China while claimed by India. Chinese military establishment clarified that India provoked Chinese army by establishing military facilities:

"In a resolute response to India's unauthorised construction of defence facilities across the border into Chinese territory in the Galwan Valley region, Chinese border soldiers have made the required moves and heightened control measures, and the Galwan Valley is Chinese territory, and the local border control situation was very clear". Analyst and commentator, Antara Ghosal Singh, (The Diplomat, 02 June 2020) has highlighted the current crisis and standpoints of both the states on Ladakh. He also noted the adoption of assertive foreign policy by China after the Pandemic. Mr. Singh argued that in Chinese strategic circles many believe that China was not "completely unrelated" to the India-Nepal border dispute, and given Nepal's strategic value to China:

> "In India, focus has been turned to the Durbuk-Shyok-Daulet Beg Oldi Road (DSBDBO) along the Galwan River—which runs more or less parallel to the LAC and improves India's access to the Karakoram Highway—as the possible trigger point for the latest flare-up between China and India. But discussions on the Chinese internet indicate that China remains much more concerned about the newly constructed 80-kilometer stretch from Dharchula to Lipulekh (the gateway to Kailash-Mansarovar, a site for Hindu pilgrimage in Tibet), completed on April 17 and inaugurated on May 8 by Indian Defense Minister Rajnath Singh. That may have led Beijing to review the situation at the China-India borders. In the Chinese assessment, India's construction activity in the disputed areas with Nepal has affected China's border security in Tibet. By building the 80 km stretch (76 km has been completed recently and the last 4 km of the road to Lipulekh Pass is expected to be completed by the year's end) India has moved it's frontier vis-a-vis China, gaining direct access to the concrete highway in Purang county in Tibet, and has thereby changed the status quo in the region. China already has border defense roads in Purang County on the middle border and Cona County on the southern border with India and a Chinese airport in Purang is scheduled to be completed in 2021. Despite its preparedness on its side of the border, China is concerned that India still has much room for maneuver, using Nepal's geographical advantage to challenge China's dominant position in the region."

On 19 January 2020, Foreign Policy noted high-level diplomatic contacts between India and China to calm tensions after a deadly skirmish between Indian and Chinese soldiers in the Ladakh border region on Monday. Indian military officials reported the clash started during a meeting attended by hundreds of soldiers on both sides who had come together along the border to discuss efforts to de-escalate tensions. Vinay Kaura (17 June 2020) has highlighted these confrontations, and noted Chinese attacks in different locations of Indian Territory:

"The face-off between Indian and Chinese forces has become uglier with the recent deaths of 20 Indian soldiers and an unknown number of Chinese soldiers. It is the first such incident in over four decades and likely to change India's perception of China decisively. US President Donald Trump initially offered to mediate to help resolve the border crisis threatening peace in the broader Himalayan region. Trump knew the two would reject his mediatory proposal. But his decision to make it should be understood within the context of his 'free and open' Indo-Pacific vision, US strategic rivalry with China, and his diplomatic aim to nudge India towards a more confrontational position vis-a-vis China. Multiple recent confrontations at different locations in eastern Ladakh along the disputed India–China boundary clearly indicate a pattern in Beijing's behaviour and some prior planning. Chinese President Xi Jinping has adopted an increasingly confrontational approach toward India, marking a new low for arguably India's most important regional relationship. And Chinese military deployment along the Line of Actual Control has been far greater than what was witnessed during the 2017 Doklam standoff. As India struggles to respond appropriately, Trump has seized the opportunity to secure a more robust commitment from India regarding its role in the Quad. Areas of tensions and divergence between India and China— boundary disputes, the China–Pakistan Economic Corridor (CPEC) and trade imbalances—seem to be manageable. But these flashpoints could turn into explosive conflicts combined. New Delhi attempted to find a modus vivendi with Beijing with informal summits between Modi and Xi in Wuhan in April 2018 and Mamallapuram in October 2019, but this is unlikely to make much of a difference, as India has often found China insensitive to its security concerns".

In May 2020, Indian and Chinese armies in physical attacks injured each other's soldiers across the disputed border, but India showed tolerance and tried to settle the issue through dialogue.

Chinese Communist army demonstrated on wrong streaks and took a stronger line and attempted to force Indian troops back. The Pakistan army may possibly support Chinese Communist Army to punish India. Walter C Ladwig (RUSI, 21 May 2020) has review altercation between the two states in his paper, and noted that China was demonstrating aggressively:

"On 5 May, India and Chinese patrols engaged in a physical altercation along their disputed border, first near Pangong Lake in Ladakh and again five days later in Sikkim, some 800 miles away. Normally such encounters are resolved by so-called 'banner drills': the defender holds their position and displays a series of signs in the other side's language informing them they are trespassing and asking them to leave. In these cases, Chinese soldiers took a stronger line and attempted to force Indian troops back, first throwing rocks, later punches. Although both episodes were resolved without a resort to deadly force, this marked the third physical confrontation at Pangong Lake in as many years and the first time patrols had confronted each other in the Sikkim sector. Moreover, both sides have reportedly reinforced their positions in the dispute zones. Do these episodes signal broader challenges for Asia's two nuclear giants? The Sino–Indian relationship is complicated. Economic ties between the two countries continue to grow. Balancing this positive development, however, is long-standing friction: tensions over the two countries' unresolved border disputes are not helped by China's continued military support for Pakistan, nor their plans to construct the China–Pakistan Economic Corridor (CPEC) through disputed territory claimed by Delhi. India's granting of sanctuary to the Dalai Lama and their hosting of the Tibetan government in exile remains a key source of mistrust from Beijing's perspective, as is New Delhi's burgeoning relationship with Washington and its steadfast refusal to join the Belt and Road Initiative (BRI)".

Analyst Bertil Lintner (18 June 2020) has highlighted growing tension between China and India, and noted Chinese warning that India can face deep challenges on three fronts. Friendly relations between Pakistan and China, and deteriorating relationship between Pakistan and India may possibly shift the war to Aksai

Chin-a remote area close to where India, China, and Pakistan meet. Pakistan is a traditional enemy of India that supports China's military operations in Ladakh. Bertil has also noted Indian military intentions in South Asia:

> "So when the official mouthpiece Global Times wrote in a June 17 commentary that India would "pay a heavy price" and "face military pressure on two or even three fronts" if it retaliated for China's killing of at least 20 Indian soldiers with rocks and spiked clubs in a Western Himalayan border altercation, the newspaper was speaking Beijing's mind. The nationalistic newspaper also wrote somewhat cryptically that "Pakistan is a reliable strategic partner of China and Nepal also has close ties with China, and both of them are key partners under the China-proposed Belt and Road Initiative", an insinuation that certain of India's neighbors could be drawn into a conflict against it if tensions escalate. Another Shanghai-based scholar quoted by Global Times reputedly said that India should not "believe that worsening China-US ties would provide a chance for India to challenge China" while suggesting any "unwise movements". could "bring about serious consequences" for India. When the border stand-off erupted earlier this month, the Global Times channeled Beijing's threat of armed conflict on June 7 by noting China had "organized a large-scale maneuver operation featuring thousands of paratroops plus armored vehicles (and) huge batches of supplies."

In South Asia, every state has applied its own classified security measures for nuclear weapons security. In Pakistan, a nuclear weapons security regime involves human, physical and technical means. However, there is a general perception that, notwithstanding these technical measures, there is a danger that nuclear materials may possibly get into the hands of terrorist organisations. The future of illicit trade of nuclear materials in South Asia by non-state actors and terrorists may further jeopardise the security of the region. The problem of this trade appears to be growing worse as technologies proliferate. With the global spread of technologies and rapid illegal sale of uranium and plutonium, traffickers could find it easier to ply their dangerous trade. If tension between the two states escalates, the possibility of nuclear war cannot be dismissed because China continues to demonstrate aggressively. India has developed more than 140 nuclear weapons, while China has developed more than 290 nuclear bombs and 320 warheads. The SIPRI report also warned that the two states are engaged in building more weapons while the two states are in border stand-off. Strait Times (16 June 2020) noted sensitivity of the looming war threat in the region:

> "Chinese nuclear forces comprise land- and sea-based ballistic missiles and aircraft that may emerge as nuclear bombers. The land- and sea-based elements are operated by the People's Liberation Army (PLA) Rocket Force, which executes nuclear strike orders issued by the Central Military Commission under Xi Jinping's chairmanship. Sea-based missiles do not have a fixed location. However, China's land-based missile bases can be geo-located. Including only the nuclear forces, and locations most relevant to targeting India.....the bases are concentrated in the far north, with three DF-21 bases in the country's south. In all, an estimated 104 Chinese missiles could strike all or parts of India. These include about a dozen DF-31A and six to twelve DF-31 missiles capable of reaching all Indian mainland targets. Another dozen DF-21s hold New Delhi at risk".

In the contemporary geopolitical landscape, the greatest threat of nuclear war is between India and Pakistan and between India and China as they possess significant nuclear arsenals consisting of short and intermediate-range ballistic missiles as well as nuclear-capable aircraft and drones. Nuclear head-to-head and ruckus between Russia, China, US, India and Pakistan has jeopardized stability and prosperity of South Asia where India has been contesting Chinese military power and Pakistan encounters India. Misinterpretation of each other's motives has also caused misunderstandings. They threaten each other with nuclear bombs and then assess its consequences and fatalities. This issue has also been highlighted in a recently published book by Nathan E Busch: "Due to continual mistrust between the two countries, each would be likely to misinterpret military movements, missiles tests, or accidental detonations as an impending attack by the other side. The risks of misinterpreting each other's motives are compounded by the vulnerabilities of their nuclear forces and the short flight times of the forces to key targets."

Pakistani Prime Minister Imran Khan who handed his government to militablishment warned of a nuclear war between India and Pakistan. In his General Assembly speech, he told the UN of potential nuclear war between the two states. Imran Khan warned that the move was driven by the Hindu nationalist ideology of the Indian Prime Minister Narendra Modi, whom he called a "fascist". The Muslim-majority territory is currently under heightened security, while mobile and internet services have been cut, but Khan predicted a popular backlash once such measures are lifted. "They'll come out on the streets. What happens then?" Khan told journalists at the UN general assembly. He pointed to the presence of a 900,000-strong Indian force enforcing security. "I fear there will be a massacre and things will start to go out of control," he said. Nuclear war could be devastating for the US as its declining global power has been challenged by China and Russia. The United States, according to some reports, has more than 3,000 nuclear weapons. The Asan Forum 25 May 2020 report noted that bioterrorism has intensified between the US and China:

"Before the ink had dried on the agreement, the epidemic had hit, casting doubt on China's ability to deliver on its promises. Washington is also conducting an ideological campaign to justify its behavior, including attacks on BRI as a debt trap and on the danger of China's 5G. China has answered these attacks. The author cites Snowden on major US companies assisting intelligence gathering by the US. China has tried to neutralize the conflict and normalize relations, stopping the trade conflict from turning into a political confrontation. Many see China as having a real chance to become a superpower, which the US seeks to prevent. Americans have long talked about containing China, but Trump is the first president to act on this. A successor could blame him, restoring relations on a peaceful track. Yet success in pressuring China will encourage the same modus operandi by Trump's successors, intensifying the containment of a geopolitical opponent. Other countries joined the US accusations, demanding more information from Beijing or permission to conduct an independent investigation. In response, Chinese diplomats and propagandists took two approaches: aggressive ("wolf warrior") nationalism and caution not to ruin relations with the establishment in the US, while praising China's role in buying time for all humanity to fight the virus and its humanitarian aid. A third direction was aggressive diplomacy to shift the blame through conspiracy theories. The target was, first of all, internal consumption to distract attention".

Keeping up the worsening war of words with Washington over the pandemic and a Beijing move to tighten control over Hong Kong, Chinese leaders warned that the United States had been infected by a "political virus" compelling figures there to continually attack China. "It has come to our attention that some political forces in the US are taking China-US relations hostage and pushing our two countries to the brink of a new Cold War," they said. Chinese military planners were aware that attempting to coerce the United States into halting conventional bombardment by alerting their nuclear forces could fail. They also know it might trigger a nuclear war. But if it does, they are equally clear China won't be the one to start it. The Trump administration is increasingly wanting to bring China into a key nuclear arms deal with Russia, according to documents obtained by Foreign Policy, amid fears by arms control experts that the effort was futile and the United States was running out of time to recommit to the Obama-era New START treaty. The growing Russian and Chinese strategic relationship is worrying. The two powers have cooperated on major energy deals, including a blockbuster $55 billion arrangement to pipe Siberian natural gas into China. However, China's missile arsenal has grown to include "carrier killers" like the DF-21D and the DF-26, which can target not only aircraft carriers and other ships over 1,000 km away, but also U.S. bases as far away as Guam.

The international community has been facing difficulties in dealing with the threat of dirty bomb, Improvised Nuclear Device and smuggling of nuclear technology since years, but after the Paris, Brussels and Pulwama attacks, experts and military commander realized that world leaders needed a joint fight against the evolved threat of nuclear terrorism. The possibility of current pandemic COVID-19 caused by Coronavirus, being a bio-weapon has caused huge fatalities and economic destruction in Europe, America and Asia. Terrorism experts are warning that the coronavirus pandemic could be used as a template for future biological attacks by either state or non-state actors. Security experts within the Council of Europe said that terrorists, assessing the impact of the coronavirus, would now recognize the fact that they could use biological weapons to inflict a major blow on Western countries. According to these experts, the virus has exposed how vulnerable modern societies are. The Council of Europe said in a statement: "The COVID-19 pandemic has demonstrated the vulnerability of modern societies to viral infections and their potential for disruption.

South Asian states are facing the threat of terrorism and violent extremism. The unending civil war in Afghanistan and Pakistan has destabilised the whole region. Terrorism in Afghanistan affects Pakistan and Iran, its heat touches the Iranian border while the flames are clearly seen in China and Russia as well. As South Asian states have been embroiled in protracted conflicts for decades, the lack of proper strategies to counter the TTP, ISIS and Indian extremism, and the clash of interests, have further aggravated the problem. Extremist and terrorist groups in this region are striving to retrieve nuclear and biological weapons and use them against the government or civilian population. The issue is further complicated as some secret reports have revealed the use of nuclear and biological weapons inside Russia. In November 1995, Chechen separatists put a crude bomb in Moscow's Izmailovsky Park.

China policy towards India in the past two decades has shifted since Indian governments supported every act of the United States against China, and constituted a commando force to halt CPEC in Ladakh and Baluchistan. India supported the Baloch national movement against Pakistan, and financed the Islamic state of Khorasan in Afghanistan. However, China advocated Jaish Muhammad, and blocked the US resolution against it. China's policy toward India has largely followed a pattern of balancing India in South Asia by propping up Pakistan and developing ties with small countries in the region. War in Afghanistan has given India a chance to destabilise Pakistan by supporting Baloch jihadist groups. Now, after the US-Taliban deal, and peace in Afghanistan (Possibly), Pakistan army and its jihadists with the support of Communist China will open a new front of Jihad against India. In this jihad, the international community will not support Pakistan and its proxies. Analyst Michael Kugelman (31 December 2019) in Foreign Policy analysis has noted the crisis in Kashmir, and Pakistan's response to the exponentially growing tension between the two states:

"In August 2019, India revoked the autonomy of Jammu and Kashmir, the India-administered part of Kashmir, and declared it a new territory of India. New Delhi also imposed a security lockdown in Kashmir that included the detention of hundreds of people and a communication blackout. For Islamabad, which claims Jammu and Kashmir as its own, the move amounted to a serious provocation, if not a hostile act. Pakistan retaliated by expelling India's envoy from Islamabad and suspending trade with New Delhi. Undaunted, in the weeks that followed, senior Indian officials—including the defense and foreign ministers—turned their attention to Pakistan-administered Kashmir, which New Delhi has long claimed, and suggested they eventually planned to reclaim it. Bilateral relations remained fraught over the last few months of the year. Islamabad issued constant broadsides against New Delhi for its continued security lockdown in Kashmir. By year's end, an internet blackout was still in effect. Then, in December, India's parliament passed a controversial new citizenship law that affords fast-track paths to Indian citizenship for religious minorities—but not Muslims—fleeing persecution in Afghanistan, Bangladesh, and Pakistan. The new law angered Islamabad not just for excluding Muslims, but because of the implication—accurate but not something Islamabad likes to admit—that Pakistan persecutes its Hindu and Christian communities. These prolonged tensions often overshadowed what was arguably the biggest story in both countries in 2019: economic struggle. India suffered its biggest economic slowdown in six years, and Pakistan confronted a serious debt crisis. The two weren't unconnected: Given the inability of New Delhi and Islamabad to fix their economies, both governments arguably sought political advantages from the distractions of saber rattling".

Chinese intervention in Gilgit Baltistan and the disputed Ladakh region has definitely exacerbated the threat of war between the two states, in which the United States and European Union may possibly support India to teach China a lesson. India probably overestimated Chinese military power, while its own wounds still need treatment in Kashmir. On August 5, 2019, the Government of India revoked the special status and limited sovereignty of Kashmir under Article 370 of the Indian Constitution. It tormented the lives of eight million people. Life is paralyzed. This lockdown of 9 months and 18 days is a telling proof not only of Kashmiris but also of human rights violations. After this operation, many attempts were made by the international human rights organizations but to no avail. Media workers were barred from working on October 3, 2019. The Internet and all other services were cut off so that they could report their situation. On August 5, 2019, the Government of India revoked the special status and limited sovereignty of Kashmir under Article 370 of the Indian Constitution.

Do Pakistan's tactical nuclear weapons (TNW) create strategic paralysis in India, for which New Delhi feels compelled to acquire nuclear counterforce options? Is development of a suite of capabilities like diverse and more delivery systems, missile defense, and surveillance platforms indicative of "India's conscious pursuit of more flexible options beyond counter value targeting?" If so, what are the implications for deterrence stability in South Asia? Will India not use the conventional forces at its disposal to resist Pakistan rather than resorting to using nuclear weapons first? Or, will India resort to a preemptive nuclear strike at once to disallow Pakistan the use of nuclear weapons first? This study delves into the nuances in vogue in the region in the contemporary strategic thinking surrounding the Indo- Pakistan nuclear discourse and the repercussions of doctrinal shifts in nuclear- use strategy regarding deterrence stability.

At present, both the states hold a massive nuclear stockpile and the size of this stockpile doubled since 1998. Both states have developed cruise missiles and are seeking nuclear submarines. China's tacit support to Pakistan for boosting the country's nuclear weapons is considered to have strategic implications for India. All these weapons and strategic developments in both states mean that confidence-building measures remain only on paper with no one wanting to extend the hand of cooperation. The main threat to Pakistan's nuclear installations might also come from a virus or worm activated within the computer. On June 9, 2014, when terrorists attacked Karachi airport and killed two military officers of the Pakistan army, the government stepped up security around nuclear installations across the country. The terrorist attack on Karachi airport showed that Pakistan's intelligence had badly failed to provide true information about terrorist networks in Karachi. This attack also highlighted the military capability of the Taliban and exposed the gap in the country's security apparatus. After this attack, Pakistanis are apprehensive about possible daring attacks against the country's nuclear installations. The terrorists yet again exposed the failure of the security agencies. This is a clear challenge for the SPD of the armed forces, which has deployed 25,000 nuclear forces around nuclear facilities.

China's economic and military power has expanded the country's political and military in South Asia, South East Asia, Europe, and in some states of Africa. The country has been investing in different projects in these states to further its national interests since years. China's military and technological power has grown during the last ten years due to the US presence in Afghanistan and the hostile attitude of the Trump administration that unexpectedly engaged it in an unending trade war. Under President Xi Jinping, China has increased its political and economic resources to build military installations in the South China Sea, fueling Washington's fears that Chinese expansionism will threaten U.S. allies and influence in the region. Moreover, deteriorating relations between China and India and military and nuclear cooperation between India and Australia also forced China to become close to Russia, and build a modern technological empire. Postgraduate student at the Department of Geopolitics and International Relations at the Manipal Academy of Higher Education in Manipal, Karnataka, India, Kanchi Mathur

(Australian Institute of International Affairs-06 JAN 2020) has viewed these developments and cooperation between India and Australia, and noted Australia's past hostile attitude towards India after the 1998 nuclear tests:

In 2014, India and Australia signed a Civil Nuclear Deal and in 2017, Australia started to make plans to supply its first uranium shipment to India. The very same year India received its first shipment of Australian uranium. Negotiations on uranium sale to India began in 2012 after Canberra lifted a long time ban on exporting the valuable ore to Delhi to meet its ambitious nuclear energy programme. Today, one of the key debates in the international community is about the deal and its future prospects for both India and Australia........India's accession to the global nuclear order to date has been incomplete. While India became a member of the Australia Group in June 2016; of the Wassenaar Agreement in July 2018; and the Missile Control Regime (MTCR) in July 2018, its hopes of membership of the NSG remains a farfetched dream. While Australia along with its godfather, the United States, continues to push for India's membership in the NSG, it is only a matter of time before Australia tones down its support of India in order to balance relations with China, which opposes the country's membership in the NSG and demands a "similar deal" with others (Pakistan); equalising India's nuclear competence with that of Pakistan. This is the paradox of being a "middle state."

The standoff between China and India, and China's military intervention in Ladakh badly affected Chinese economy, and its image in the international community. Chinese army killed 20 Indian soldiers on the pretext that they had provoked the country by crossing the border illegally. India was defeated in the war in 1962. China also supports Pakistan in its own disputes with India, and China's CPEC has stirred Indian fears. Analysts James Palmer and Ravi Agrawal (16 June 2020) in their paper highlighted recent skirmishes in historical perspective:

"Despite their early friendship in the 1950s, relations between India and China rapidly degenerated over the unresolved state of their Himalayan border. The border lines, largely set by British surveyors, are unclear and heavily disputed—as was the status of Himalayan kingdoms such as Tibet, Sikkim, Bhutan, and Nepal. That led to a short war in 1962, won by China. China also backs Pakistan in its own disputes with India, and China's Belt and Road Initiative has stirred Indian fears, especially the so-called China-Pakistan Economic Corridor, a collection of large infrastructure projects. The current border is formally accepted by neither side but simply referred to as the Line of Actual Control. In 2017, an attempt by Chinese engineers to build a new road through the disputed territory on the Bhutan-India-China border led to a 73-day standoff on the Doklam Plateau, including fistfights between Chinese and Indian soldiers. Following Doklam, both countries built new military infrastructure along the border. India, for example, constructed roads and bridges to improve its connectivity to the Line of Actual Control, dramatically improving its ability to bring in emergency reinforcements in the event of a skirmish. In early May this year, a huge fistfight along the border led to both sides boosting local units, and there have been numerous light skirmishes—with no deaths—since then. Both sides have accused the other of deliberately crossing the border on numerous occasions. Until Monday's battle, however, diplomacy seemed to be slowly de-escalating the crisis".

After the Chinese army attacked Indian army soldiers in a hand to hand fight that left 20 Indian soldiers dead, Prime Minister Modi warned that the sacrifice made by the soldiers would not go in vain. Minister of External Affairs S Jaishankar spoke to his Chinese counterpart Wang Yi. Former Congress president Rahul Gandhi, meanwhile, said the country needs more clarity on what was happening. India and Pakistan have developed advanced missile technology, and tested short and long range nuclear and non-nuclear missiles. Research Affiliate at the Strategic Vision Institute (SVI), a non-partisan think-tank based out of Islamabad, Pakistan, Sher Bano (16 June 2020) has reviewed rapid modernization of India and Pakistan, and noted their frustration and fear of each other military build up:

"The rapid modernization of strategic weapons in South Asia has become the cause of increasing rivalry between India and Pakistan. With India's quest to achieve a nuclear triad that includes the development of submarine launched ballistic missile, land based ballistic missiles and fighter bomber aircrafts; it aspires to attain the global power status. India in order to strengthen its nuclear force is rigorously working on building a strong naval force and is also developing short range ballistic missiles that are nuclear in nature. India is also expanding its capabilities in outer space by developing its fleet of satellites and is building anti-satellite missiles that can be used for both military and civilian purposes. This shift in India's nuclear posture along with strategic modernization will pose a huge threat to Pakistan's nuclear threshold and will increase the risk of nuclear escalation in South Asia. On January 8, top Government officials of India said "The BMD program has been completed". Under this program India has developed homegrown ballistic missile defense (BMD). DRDO and IAF are now looking for the government's approval in order to activate and install the system. But according to the sources the complete installation of the system will still take three to four years..

The misinterpretation of each other's motives has also caused misunderstandings. First, they threaten each other with nuclear bombs and then assess the consequences and fatalities. This issue has also been highlighted in a recently published book by Nathan E Busch: "Due to continual mistrust between the two countries, each would be likely to misinterpret military movements, missiles tests, or accidental detonations as an impending attack by the other side. In his General Assembly speech, Imran Khan warned the UN of potential nuclear war in Kashmir. Imran Khan warned that the move was driven by the Hindu nationalist ideology of the Indian Prime Minister Narendra Modi, whom he called a "fascist". The Muslim-majority territory is currently under heightened security, while mobile and internet services have been cut, but Khan predicted a popular backlash once such measures are lifted. "They'll come out on the streets. What happens then?" Khan told journalists at the UN general assembly. He pointed to the presence of a 900,000-strong Indian force there currently enforcing security.

Analysts Sanjana Gogna and Nasima Khatoon, (March 27, 2020) in their paper noted Chinese military and nuclear assistance to Pakistan, and 1980, China transferred the entire nuclear design to Pakistan, and provided Pakistan with weapon-grade uranium that could power two nuclear devices:

"The incident at Kandla port signals that Chinese assistance to Pakistan remains a cause of concern for India, as Islamabad has been rapidly advancing its nuclear weapons capabilities with China's help. Of late, Pakistan has introduced several new nuclear-capable missile systems such as the solid-fuel ballistic missile Shaheen III, which has a range of 2,750 km. Experts have identified significant similarities between the designs of Shaheen missiles and China's DF-11. Plus, in March 2018, the Defense Intelligence Agency of the United States confirmed that Pakistan had conducted tests of a Multiple Independent Reentry Vehicles (MIRV) capable missile, Ababeel. MIRV capability allows a ballistic missile to send several separately targeted nuclear warheads on their separate ways. China later confirmed its assistance to Pakistan in developing MIRV capabilities, which included the sale of a highly sophisticated, large-scale optical tracking and measurement system. The Indian government, in addition to seizing the autoclave aboard the Dai Cui Yun as per domestic legal procedures, has conveyed its concern to the Chinese side; both actions demonstrate India's proactive stand against China's nuclear proliferation. However, it is crucial for India to use other diplomatic options to counter the China-Pakistan nuclear nexus".

Border tensions between Beijing and New Delhi have been developing since months as troops from both sides are engaged in clashes despite Chinese and Indian military generals meeting to defuse the crisis. Zoe Jordan, in his China-US Focus analysis, (03 February, 2020) argued that tension between India and china may possibly escalate into a major conflict, but noted that as the two states maintain a bigger nuclear arsenals, they can return to their borders and settle the issue by entering a composite dialogue: "Tensions between India and China will undoubtedly continue, and disputes are unlikely to be resolved quickly or easily. But few can legitimately argue that these disputes are likely to escalate into high-level conflict. As such, the type of deterrence established between India and China—two countries with a significant amount of problem solving to undertake, who maintain nuclear arsenals poised at one another, and who nonetheless are in little danger of accidentally falling into nuclear war—should be an example for policymakers to seek lessons in deterrence".

Musa Khan Jalalzai

July 2020, London

Modern Nuclear Technology and the Danger of Nuclear War in South Asia

After the cold war, emergence of the United States as a global economic and military power, and its challenge of global dominance by Russia and China in the 1990s-the two big powers became close to prevent political and military influence of the United States in Southeast Asia, South Asia and Central Asia. During the last 20 years, President Putin reorganized Russia into a strong military and democratic power-built his strongest army and innovated modern nuclear and non-nuclear weapons to defend the territorial integrity of his country. China and Russia developed new weapons to intercept US aggression against states on its periphery under the cover of increasingly capable reconnaissance-strike networks. The geographic friction points in the Western Pacific and Eastern Europe that is most likely to devolve into crisis and conflict lie much closer to Russia and China than they do to the continental United States. In their well-written paper, Thomas G. Mahnken Travis Sharp Grace B.KIM (2020) have highlighted in detail competition between Russia and the United States:

"The U.S. armed forces are poorly configured to meet these challenges, which require long duration monitoring rather than episodic coverage. Although the Defense Department has the requisite existing and near-term capabilities to do so, namely non-stealthy long-endurance UAS, it needs to develop new concepts of operations and organizations to employ those capabilities effectively. The new concept for employing UAS to deter opportunistic aggression, which we call "deterrence by detection," will also benefit greatly from approaches that allow allies and partners to participate fully. Today and for the foreseeable future, the most important and consequential challenge facing the United States and its allies will be the need to compete with, deter, and potentially fight China and Russia. This strategic imperative translates into a series of operational challenges that are the result of a combination of the tyranny of distance and eroding military balances. Although the Pacific and Atlantic oceans protect the United States against attack, the immense distance between North America and the European and Asian continents guarantees that the objects of Chinese or Russian aggression lie closer to them than to the United States. Delivering military force across the Pacific and Atlantic oceans has never been easy, even for a country as powerful as the United States."[1]

Russian Television (RT) in 2014 aired an interview of Wikileaks founder Mr. Julian Assange with a UK based Australian journalist, Mr. John Pilger. Mr. Assange uncovered important facts about the wealthy officials from Saudi Arabia and Qatar donating money to the Hillary Clinton's Foundation and Islamic State (IS) respectively. On 17 August 2014, Mr. Assange made public an email in which Hillary Clinton urged the then advisor to US President Barack Obama, Mr. John Podesta, to pressure Qatar and Saudi Arabia for funding Islamic State (ISIS). These revelations sparked wide-ranging debates in print and electronic media across the globe, which affected relations of the Qatar and Saudi governments with the Gulf and South Asian states. It is alleged that Saudi financial assistance to extremist organisations prompted unprecedented civil wars, devastation, torture and displacement of millions of Muslims in Middle East, South Asia, and Gulf regions. Similar rumours are at spin regarding the militant Islamic group Daesh. There are different opinions about the strength and area of Daesh's influence, but recent events proved that Daesh is more powerful than the Taliban terrorist groups.[2]

With the establishment of Islamic State (ISIS) in Syria and Iraq and its secret networks and propaganda campaign in Pakistan and Afghanistan, the international community has now focused on the proliferation and smuggling of chemical and biological weapons in the region. The recent debate in Europe-based think tanks suggests that, as the group retrieved nuclear and biological material from the Mosul University in Iraq, it can possibly make nuclear explosive devices with less than eight kilograms plutonium. The debate about bioterrorism and biodefense is not entirely new in the military circles of South Asia; the involvement of IS in using biological weapons against the Kurdish army in Kobane is a lesson for Pakistan and Afghanistan to deeply concentrate on the proliferation of these weapons in the region.

There were different perceptions that future wars will wipe out geographical and social stratification of some states in South Asia and Persian Gulf because modern technologies are continuing to influence the nature of nuclear war in these regions. The possible drawdown of US forces and the Patriot Missiles system from Saudi Arabia may possibly encourage Iran to extend its political and military influence in both Persian Gulf and Middle East regions. However, Russia is a leading power in developing new military technologies, while President Vladimir Putin once said that modern equipment made up 82 percent of Russia's nuclear triad: "our equipment must be better than the world's best if we want to come out as the winners."

The different modalities of nuclear or radiological terrorism include: an attack on a nuclear facility, theft of nuclear or radiological material and construction of a "dirty bomb," and theft of a nuclear weapon. Experts emphasize that the risk of allies rapidly nuclearizing is low. Moreover, that risk will grow. Modern military technologies have changed the effectiveness of operations in the battlefields. The use of some newly invented weapons in Afghanistan, Syria and Iraq added to the pain of civil society in Russia, and Europe. The introduction and use of these technologies is understood as a series of qualitative changes in mobilisation of bigger armies. Security Forces have become technologically complex. Analysts Maxim Suchkov, Sim Tack (The Future of War, Valdai Discussion Club Report, August 2019) have noted some important aspects of modern future war and its impacts on modern society:

"The evolution of technologies is the first and perhaps main element where public perceptions are concerned. However, with all their importance, technologies are only able to foster change in tandem with other components. Their emergence and subsequent introduction in the armed forces facilitates the development of relevant skills and capabilities, which in turn stimulate the emergence of new procedures to harness their potential. The political antagonisms of the modern world have reached a degree that is indeed alarming. No less destabilizing than the lowered pain threshold that used to guard against the use of force or wars between the states – is the visible imbalance between the advancing technological warfare capabilities and the lack of practical experience in using these technologies. This is one of the reasons why the contours of a large-scale military clash between major or comparable powers are still unclear."[3]

These technological developments of Russian military industry are intolerable for the US administration that used nuclear bombs and missiles against the civilian population of Afghanistan, which caused incurable diseases. Russia has made good progress, and emerged as the strongest nuclear and military superpower. A superpower emerged with national unity, resolve and well-trained army that challenged hegemonic designs of the United States across Europe and Asia. Emerging market of Russian weapons and nuclear power reactors has put in trouble the US military industry and political leadership. Ben Aris (08 May 2019) has highlighted the Russian weapons market from India to Africa, and its effectiveness of nuclear weapons in war and peace:

"In recent years Rosatom has completed the construction of six nuclear power reactors in India, Iran and China and it has another nine reactors under construction in Turkey, Belarus, India, Bangladesh and China. Rosatom confirmed to bne IntelliNews that it has a total of 19 more "firmly planned" projects and an additional 14 "proposed" projects, almost all in emerging markets around the world. Rosatom has become the world's largest nuclear reactor builder as the financial problems of the two big Western firms Westinghouse Areva have crimped their ability to develop nuclear plants abroad. Westinghouse and Areva, now owned by

EDF, have for year's negotiated deals to build reactors in India but have made little progress, partly because Indian nuclear liability legislation gives reactor manufacturers less protection against claims for damages in case of accidents. The sales drive was organised by former Prime Minister Sergei Kiriyenko, who presided over Russia during the 1998 financial crisis but was given the job of running Rosatom after leaving office and tasked with selling 40 nuclear power plants internationally. The world just marked the thirtieth anniversary of the Chernobyl disaster on April 26, however, those ill-fated RBMK-type reactors have long ago been ditched and replaced by the third generation VVER 1200 (water-water energetic reactor) that are compliant with the IAEA's International Nuclear Safety Group (INSAG) recommendations and general considered to be safe. Part of Rosatom's appeal is not only Russia's lower prices and state-of-the-art technology but the fact that the company usually provides most of the financing for the typically $10bn price tag".[4]

Recent warning of the Putin administration against the US low-yield nuclear weapon indicates that Russian forces are capable of destroying US Submarines in a short notice. On 29 April 2020; VOA reported reaction of Russian Foreign Ministry to the State Department paper assertion that the low-yield weapons "reduce the risk of nuclear war by reinforcing extended deterrence and assurance".[5] Moreover, Federation of American Scientists warned (January 2020) that the U.S. Navy had deployed for the first time a submarine armed with a low-yield Trident Nuclear Warhead.[6] However, on 16 April 2020, Associated Press reported Chinese Foreign Ministry response to the allegations of U.S. State Department report about the country's secret nuclear test: "China has always performed its international obligations and commitments in a responsible manner, firmly upheld multilateralism, and actively carried out international cooperation," Foreign Minister Spokeswoman said.[7]

The Trump administration is in deep trouble since the test of Russia's anti-satellite missiles and its defeat in Afghanistan. NATO and the United States issued warnings of the Russian hybrid war in Europe, but they continue to destabilise Middle East and Central Asia and used nuclear and biological weapons in Iraq and Afghanistan. However, the EU member states are well aware of their security and friendship with Russia by extending a hand of cooperation due to the hegemonic attitude of the Trump administration. In this big strategic game, Russians and Americans have the same reason for modernizing their nuclear forces. In yesteryears, President Vladimir Putin developed modern weapons and restored the real Russian place in the international community. Since Russia seized Crimea in 2014, Russians have begun to build up basing sites for their advanced systems, including the Iskanders, but nuclear experts warned that if Russia deploys nuclear weapons there, it will spark complex problems. Analyst Scott Ritter (RT News, 28 April 2020) highlighted the START and complication of US and Russia's inventions of modern technologies and weapons, which will exacerbate the process of nuclear war preparations:

"Both the US and Russia are engaged in the early stages of developing new strategic nuclear weapons to replace older systems. These weapons, which will cost trillions of dollars to develop and deploy, are with few exceptions still many years away from entering into service. A five-year extension of New START would provide both nations time to reach an agreement which responsibly addresses the need for strategic nuclear force modernization while continuing the past practice of seeking additional cuts in their respective nuclear arsenals........China's intransigence runs counter to the official US position, most recently articulated in a State Department report sent to Congress regarding Russian compliance with the New START Treaty. While the report finds that Russia is complying with its treaty obligations, the treaty does not cover enough Russian strategic systems, including several that have been previously announced by President Putin, and leaves China to operate with no restrictions in terms of the size and scope of its strategic nuclear arsenal".[8]

Perhaps, China is also preparing to build new missile technology, expand anti-satellite capabilities and increase nuclear material production. The question is how China can use nuclear weapons as the country maintains the policy of peaceful coexistence? In 2019, its Defence White Paper noted the country stuck to the policy of no first use of nuclear weapons at any time and under any circumstances, but the recent hostile nuclear environment has forced the country to deploy a nuclear triad of strategic land, sea, and air-launched nuclear systems to defend its territorial integrity and national security. Despite the progress made by international conventions, biological and chemical weapons are still a precarious threat in Europe and Central Asia. In his Asia Times article, Richard Javad Heydarian (25 May 2020) has noted the US and China confrontations, quoted Pentagon report about the attitude of the Chinese government:

"In a recent report to the US Congress entitled "United States Strategic Approach to the People's Republic of China", Trump's White House argues that "Beijing contradicts its rhetoric and flouts its commitments to its neighbours by engaging in provocative and coercive military and paramilitary activities in the Yellow Sea, the East and South China Seas, the Taiwan Strait, and Sino-Indian border areas." Submitted in compliance with the National Defense Authorization Act 2019, which mandates a comprehensive approach to dealing with China's perceived threat, the report warned that China has shown "the willingness and capacity…to employ intimidation and coercion in its attempts to eliminate perceived threats to its interests and advance its strategic objectives globally." Portraying Beijing as an expansionist power, the report also argues that China's recent behavior in the South China Sea and other contested waters "belie Chinese leaders' proclamations that they oppose the threat or use of force, do not intervene in other countries' internal affairs, or are committed to resolving disputes through peaceful dialogue." As part of a broader containment strategy, the US is also seeking the support of other regional powers including India to ringfence China's naval ambitions in the South China Sea and beyond. During a recent public talk in Washington, Alice Wells, the outgoing Principal Deputy Assistant Secretary of State for South and Central Asian Affairs, called on regional partners to resist China's "constant aggression, the constant attempt to shift the norms, to shift what is the status quo".[9]

In Europe, there is the general perception that IS has already used some dangerous gases in Iraq. Therefore, it could use biological weapons against civilian populations in Pakistan. If control over these weapons is weak, or if their components are available in the open market, there would be huge destruction in the region. In July 2014, the government of Iraq notified that nuclear material had been seized by the IS army from Mosul University. IS has a 19-page document in Arabic on how to develop biological weapons, and a 26-page religious fatwa that allows the use of weapons of mass destruction. "If Muslims cannot defeat the kafir (non-believers) in a different way, it is permissible to use weapons of mass destruction," warns the fatwa.

The effects of chemical weapons are worse as they cause death or incapacitation, while biological weapons cause death or disease in humans, animals or plants. We have two international treaties that ban the use of such weapons. Notwithstanding all these preventive measures, the threat of chemical or biological warfare persists. In 2011 and 2013, there were complaints and allegations that some states wanted to target Pakistan with biological weapons. The country has been trying to counter biological attacks but has failed due to limited funds and medical knowledge. As Pakistan noted in its statement to the Meeting of States Parties in December 2013: "Pakistan ratified the Biological and Toxic Weapons Convention (BTWC) in 1974 as a non-possessor state and remains fully committed to implementing all provisions of the convention."

The fatalities of dengue and ebola viruses in Pakistan and West Africa are the worst forms of bioterrorism. In 2011, the Pakistan Medical Association called on the ISI to investigate fears of the deliberate spread of the deadly disease in Punjab. There are speculations that, in future, measles, dengue, polio and the ebola viruses can be used as weapons of bioterrorism in Pakistan. Some states might use drones for the purposes of bio-war against their rival states. In 2013, writing in the Global Policy Journal, Amanda M Teckman warned that IS might possibly use ebola as a weapon against the civilian population: "It remains to be seen if a terrorist group like IS, which has demonstrated a willingness to engage in large scale mass murder, including the uninhibited murder of civilians, has the capability to produce a weaponised version of ebola." The University of Birmingham Policy Commission Report warned that terrorists could also turn remotely piloted aircraft into flying bombs by hooking them up to improvised explosive devices. Sir David, a former British intelligence researcher, warned that drones had gained a reputation as unaccountable killing machines because of their widespread use in the US's controversial anti-terrorist campaigns in Pakistan, Yemen and Somalia.[10]

According to Russia's new military doctrine the possibility of limited uses of nuclear weapons at the tactical and operational levels and of chemical and biological weapons is possible. As the United States and NATO have established biological weapons laboratories in Central Asia and Afghanistan and used these weapons against the civilian population of Afghanistan, Russian military leadership has taken these developments seriously. Russia is training its chemical and biological army on a modern streak. New CBRN defense vehicles and equipment can be used in the fight against coronavirus. Its forces have also undertaken more CBRN training to the future war effectively. The danger from these weapons is so consternating, and the dirty bomb material and its fatalities diverted the attention of terrorist groups to biological weapons. Smuggling of nuclear weapons is a serious challenge in Europe and Central Asia, while smuggling of these weapons in Africa and Europe has threatened the security of the region.

The terror attacks in Brussels also punctuated the issue of nuclear security, when Belgian authorities discovered ISIS was conducting surveillance of a local nuclear scientist and his family. The fear of Pakistani nuclear weapons falling into terrorists' hands has existed since the 1990s. In an article in the New York Times in April 2017 Rahmatullah Nabil, the former head of Afghan intelligence, claimed that internal Pakistani classified documents had expressed concerns regarding terrorists' threats to the country's nuclear assets. However, on 18 May 2020, TASS News reported Russian Deputy Foreign Minister Sergey Ryabkov that the deployment of US land-based intermediate-and shorter-range missiles in Europe after their deployment in the Asia-Pacific region was possible:

"However, in their reply, they let us know that they did not intend to follow our example and would not introduce a moratorium on the deployment of their new missiles. By all indications, their corresponding test programs will be activated in the short term and subsequently, such systems may begin to be deployed on the ground," Ryabkov said. On August 2, 2019, the Intermediate-Range Nuclear Forces (INF) Treaty was officially terminated at the US initiative.[11] The US claimed that its actions were provoked by Russia's refusal to comply with the American ultimatum-like demand to eliminate the new 9M729 cruise missiles, which, as Washington and its NATO allies believe, violate the INF Treaty. Moreover, on 18 May 2020, RT News reported an escalation of US-China hostility. However, TAAS news agency reported deployment of a batch of six Project 22800 missile corvettes, armed with the Kalibr cruise missiles in the Baltic Fleet:

"Soon, the surface part of the Baltic Fleet will be reinforced with a batch of six Project 22800 missile corvettes. Four of them will carry a naval version of the Pantsir system. Odintsovo will become the first one, the Pantsir system will undergo testing on this ship," the Commander's congratulatory telegram to the sailors, dedicated to the Fleet's 317th anniversary, says, according to the Fleet press service. The Project 22800 corvettes are equipped with Kalibr cruise missiles, modern control, radio, navigation, electronic warfare systems, counter-diversion armaments, man-portable air-defense systems. The ships are designed to act either as part of naval groups or on their own.[12]

According to a new US report, there are record levels of opium production in the country, which is now a three billion dollar industry with much of the profit going to the Taliban and Afghan parliamentarians. Parliamentarians, the police, ministers, secret agencies and the national army are not interested in stabilising their country. The Soviet-influenced Afghan intelligence agencies have no roots in the south, east and southwest of the country. They are unable to collect true intelligence information from 50 percent of the area of Afghanistan. They are corrupt, jingoist, incompetent and facilitate terrorist networks. In view of the Taliban's increasingly bold attacks in Kabul, last Sunday, the president of the unity government angrily criticised the failure of intelligence, and announced reviving the old sovietised intelligence infrastructure. However, Pakistan's long sustained policy of appeasing proxies and jihadists also caused instability in Afghanistan. Terrorism operations have been legitimised in the country by Pakistan, which supports the 'good' Taliban and hammers the 'bad' Taliban.

The threat of nuclear weapons theft and bioterrorism in South Asia once again came under discussion in the international press on how terrorist organisations in both Pakistan and India are trying to retrieve biotechnology and nuclear weapons, and use them against civilians and the security forces. The recent border skirmishes between Pakistan and India, the cloud of civil war in Afghanistan and the emergence of the Islamic State of Iraq and Syria (ISIS) terrorist organisation in the Persian Gulf and the Arab world further justified the possibilities of the complex threat of chemical and biological terrorism. As Pakistan and Afghanistan have been the victims of terrorism and Talibanisation during the last three decades, the establishment of ISIS networks in South Asia may possibly change the traditional concept of terrorism and insurgency in the region.

There is a general perception that extremist organisations in South Asia could use some advanced technologies against civilian populations. If control over these weapons is weak, the possibility of theft increases. The problem of nuclear and biological terrorism deserves special attention from all South Asian states, including Afghanistan. Like nuclear weapons, missile technologies and bio-weapons proliferate, there is a grave danger that some of them might fall into the hands of the Pakistani Taliban (TTP), ISIS and Indian and Afghani extremist groups. In South and Central Asia, some states, including Pakistan, have started responding to the threat of nuclear and biological terrorism with technical means.

Each state has its own approach towards the threat perception. The more recent focus on global terrorism issues is also now sharpening the focus on non-proliferation activities that do not necessarily apply at the level of the state. There are speculations that non-state actors might possibly engage in these activities. The Islamic State that controls parts of Iraq and Syria has established its network in Afghanistan and Pakistan as the region is already dominated by violent terrorist groups. The New York Times recently reported that as many as 1,000 Turks joined the ISIS network. The CIA estimated last week that the group had anywhere from 20,000 to 31,500 fighters in Iraq and Syria.

South Asian states are facing the threat of terrorism and violent extremism. The unending civil war in Afghanistan and Pakistan has destabilised the whole region. Terrorism in Afghanistan affects Pakistan and Iran, its heat touches the Iranian border while the flames are clearly seen in China and Russia as well. As South Asian states have been embroiled in protracted conflicts for decades, the lack of proper strategies to counter the TTP, ISIS and Indian extremism, and the clash of interests, have further aggravated the problem. Extremist and terrorist groups in this region are striving to retrieve nuclear and biological weapons and use them against the government or civilian population. The issue is further complicated as some secret reports have revealed the use of nuclear and biological weapons inside Russia. In November 1995, Chechen separatists put a crude bomb in Moscow's Izmailovsky Park.

The debate about bioterrorism is not entirely new in the region because both Pakistan and India have developed these weapons to use them in a future war. On December 3, 1984, the worst chemical disaster occurred in the city of Bhopal in India, causing the deaths of thousands of people. If a nuclear war were to break out in South Asia, experts believe that it is most likely to happen in India and Pakistan. This kind of war would have dire consequences. In the Seoul Summit, Indian Prime Minister Manmohan Singh warned that South Asia is under threat. Two incidents in Karachi and another in Balochistan proved that terrorists were trying to retrieve nuclear weapons to use them against military or nuclear installations.

The Indian government has recognised the threat from bioweapons as real and imminent. Both the ministry of defence and ministry of home affairs placed high priority on this issue. India understands that Pakistan-based terrorist groups may possibly use these weapons in Kashmir in the near future. Pakistan too has expressed deep concern about the use of these weapons against its security forces either by the Taliban or Baloch insurgents. The emergence of recent polio and bird flu cases in Pakistan is the primary warning of danger. The nucleation of my debate on nuclear terrorism is that, once the TTP or other terrorist group steals biological and nuclear weapons, they will use them against the military and nuclear installations. National security experts in the UK and US believe that the most likely way terrorists will obtain a nuclear bomb will not be to steal or purchase a fully operational device but to buy fissile material and construct their own.

In South Asia, every state has applied its own classified security measures for nuclear weapons security. In Pakistan, a nuclear weapons security regime involves human, physical and technical means. However, there is a general perception that, notwithstanding these technical measures, there is a danger that nuclear materials may possibly get into the hands of terrorist organisations. The future of illicit trade of nuclear materials in South Asia by non-state actors and terrorists may further jeopardise the security of the region. The problem of this trade appears to be growing worse as technologies proliferate. With the global spread of technologies and rapid illegal sale of uranium and plutonium, traffickers could find it easier to ply their dangerous trade.

The absence of available reports in official data does not negate the fact the terrorist and extremist organisations interact in the smuggling of nuclear materials. India and Pakistan understand the sensitivity of the protection of these weapons. By analysing the threat of chemical and bioterrorism in South Asia, I do not want to exaggerate or distort facts.

Chapter-2

Pakistan's Nuclear Weapons, Kashmir and India

Global concern over nuclear terrorism in South Asia and Europe has grown during the past few decades. In yesteryears, the prospect of extremists armed with dirty bomb materials has frequently been cited as a genuine and overriding threat to the security of South Asia. How is it possible for terrorist groups to use these weapons against the armed forces of the region, and how can they constitute material of dirty bombs? Having answered these questions, senior analyst Evan B. Montgomery has noted some aspects of nuclear and biological terrorism:

How real is the risk that a terrorist group could acquire or construct a functional nuclear device, and how might it attempt to do so? Which group poses the greatest threat in this regard, how has that threat changed over time, and is it currently growing or abating? What existing and prospective measures will prove most effective in preventing terrorists from obtaining a nuclear weapon, stopping them from delivering and detonating a weapon if prevention fails, and responding both at home and abroad in the event that an attack succeeds? The purpose of this backgrounder is to examine these critical issues. There are two major dimensions of the nuclear terrorist threat: the "supply" side of nuclear proliferation and the "demand" side of violent Islamist extremism. Over the past decade, longstanding concerns over proliferation have become increasingly acute in light of a number of worrisome developments, including the status of India and Pakistan as overt nuclear-weapon states."[1]

The continued nuclear weapons build up in India and Pakistan, and their unnecessary confrontation on Kashmir is a threat to peace and stability of South Asia. Recent threats of using nuclear weapons against each other has prompted deep anxiety in the neighbouring states that the use of nuclear bombs would also affect their social, economic and health sectors. In the contemporary geopolitical landscape, the greatest threat of nuclear exchange between the two states has created a climate of fear as they possess significant nuclear arsenals consisting of short and intermediate range ballistic missiles as well as nuclear-capable aircraft. Mahmudul Huque (1 February 2020) highlighted this way of confrontation between the two states:

"Their eventual nuclearization gave them the status of nuclear states which constituted a significant erosion of the nonproliferation norms as stipulated by both these treaties aimed at nuclear disarmament. Pakistan's position in this regard was quite straightforward, offering to sign the treaties if India did the same. New Delhi, however, looked upon the NPT regime as discriminatory as it formalized two categories of states in the world: the legitimate nuclear weapons states (NWS) and the non-nuclear weapons states (NNWS). India considers the NPT regime as a "thinly disguised form of 'nuclear apartheid,' intended to ensure the dominance of the few over the many in the international system." India also considered Pakistan's offer to sign the NPT a bluff. But, according to the Asia Society Study Group Report, "it is a bluff New Delhi has been unwilling to call." The perennial India-Pakistan hostility over Kashmir is one of the major reasons for India-Pakistan arms race—whether conventional or nuclear. India's enmity with China, especially after its defeat in the 1962 Sino-India War, is also a great security concern for New Delhi."[2]

In June 2015, Indian security forces carried out military operations against insurgents in Myanmar, which caused tension between India and Pakistan when Indian leaders warned that it could happen in Pakistan as well. Prime Minister Nawaz Sharif and Defence Minister Khwaja Asif responded with strong words. Asif warned India that Pakistan was a nuclear state and the country does not maintain a nuclear bomb just to use it as a firecracker.

"If forced into war by India, Pakistan will respond in a befitting manner; our arms are not meant for decoration," he said. Former president General Musharraf also responded aggressively in turn, saying that Pakistan would adopt a tit-for-tat approach and would react immediately: "Don't attack us, don't challenge our territorial integrity because we are not a small power, we are a major nuclear power."[3]

The issue of nuclear terrorism in South Asia has become very complicated, as both India and Pakistan threaten each other with an attack by nuclear weapons. On February 28, 2015, the US government warned about the possibility of an Indian nuclear attack on Pakistan if terrorists attacked India. Recently, in the US Senate, government officials and researchers warned that in case of an Indian attack, Pakistan would use nuclear weapons against the country. "South Asia is the most likely place nuclear weapons could be detonated in the foreseeable future. This risk derives from the unusual dynamic of the India-Pakistan competition," Carnegie researcher Perkovich said.

However, General Khalid Kidwai, a former Director-General of the Strategic Planning Division of Pakistan remarked that Pakistan had enough nuclear weapons to ensure that a war in the subcontinent was no longer an option. His remarks appeared to suggest that the nuclear deterrence debate in this region has been settled. General Kidwai implicitly acknowledged that Pakistan used extremist groups as foreign policy instruments. He blamed the crisis in Kashmir and Afghanistan to justify Pakistan's actions. Deterrence is not a condition achieved from simply possessing nuclear weapons; it is based on the perception of military power in general. Nuclear weapons drastically enhance a state's strength by creating the capacity to cause catastrophic amounts of damage in a very short period of time, with strikes that are largely indefensible. Mahmudul Huque (01 February 2028) noted weaknesses of both states to end the crisis. However, he views this unending confrontation as an evolving threat of nuclear war:

"In South Asia, Pakistan is the revisionist power and would start the conflict to upset the status quo." This analyst points out a very potent flaw in Pakistan's drawing the red-line at which India should stop or otherwise be prepared for Pakistan's nuclear reprisal. As he mentions, "India does not really know where this mythical line called the nuclear threshold is situated and would disbelieve any 'early' attempt by Pakistan to declare that the threshold has been reached. This is exactly what happened during the Kargil crisis when junior ministers in Pakistan were obviously primed to say that the threshold had been reached." Flaws of Deterrence, therefore, based on the experiences of the India-Pakistan conflicts that occurred after the two countries became nuclear capable, one cannot rule out the possibility of a nuclear exchange between the two countries. Their doctrinal preferences, engendering mutual miscalculations, reinforce this danger. Moreover, deterrence is far from foolproof in South Asia. Particularly, Pakistan's reliance on preventing Indian conventional attack with nuclear deterrence may prove dangerous. If India crosses the Pakistani thresholds, even unintentionally, and Pakistan uses nuclear weapons, the latter is certain to retaliate in kind and inflict unacceptable damage on Pakistan. Indian doctrine emphasizes a retaliatory strike against any nuclear attack."[4]

Construction of new nuclear power plants in Pakistan raised some questions that by expanding its nuclear installations network, Pakistan does not comply with the principles of the International Atomic Energy Agency (IAEA) non-proliferation policy. Having ignored international concerns on nuclear power plants, the Environmental Protection Agency of Sindh province approved the twin nuclear project and allowed its construction. Now, as both the states are nuclear powers, Pakistan recognises that terrorist attacks from its territory against India are not in its interest. In fact, the access of terrorist groups to fissile materials in both states is evident from the fact that the safety and security of nuclear sites in India is not satisfactory. The same question arises in Pakistan, where party politics in the Atomic Energy Commission and a lack of civilian oversight has received deep criticism from the world's media.

The threat of chemical, biological and nuclear terrorism in South Asia also causes deep frustration and anxiety, as the region hosts many militant organisations. These groups have already learnt the technique of making nuclear explosive devices and the illegal transactions of poorly protected materials remain a threat. The Subcontinent is the most volatile region because India and Pakistan are engaged in a dangerous nuclear arms race. India is enjoying conventional superiority. The addition of a nuclear dimension to this conflict is a matter of great concern. India's National Security Advisor admitted in one of his recent speeches that a fourth-generation war is being fought against Pakistan with different tactics and dimensions. Strategically speaking, India and Pakistan have their own threat perceptions, which are quite similar. India wants to be a strong nuclear state because of its fear of Chinese aggression, while Pakistan also needs nuclear weapons because of its fear of Indian aggression. China helps Pakistan in upgrading its nuclear weapons and provides sophisticated weapons to the country's army, while the US helps India.

The misinterpretation of each other's motives has also caused misunderstandings. First, they threaten each other with nuclear bombs and then assess the consequences and fatalities. This issue has also been highlighted in a recently published book by Nathan E Busch: "Due to continual mistrust between the two countries, each would be likely to misinterpret military movements, missiles tests, or accidental detonations as an impending attack by the other side. The risks of misinterpreting each other's motives are compounded by the vulnerabilities of their nuclear forces and the short flight times of the forces to key targets."[5]

The jihadist organisations in South Asia, and even the Islamic State (ISIS) and Taliban, have already demonstrated their interest in retrieving chemical and nuclear weapons, but at present, there is no evidence of their attempts to get access to these weapons. IS recently claimed that it is engaged with Pakistan for nuclear weapons delivery, but this cannot be confirmed through any research papers or news reports. There are confirmed reports that IS retrieved chemical weapons from Iraq and jihadist groups in South Asia are struggling to obtain chemical weapons capability. In summation, as both India and Pakistan are responsible nuclear states, they need to avoid misinterpreting each other's motives and share such intelligence information that could help prevent nuclear incidents.

Pakistani Prime Minister Imran Khan who handed his government to militablishment wants a nuclear war between India and Pakistan. In his General Assembly speech, he warned the UN of potential nuclear war in Kashmir. Imran Khan warned that the move was driven by the Hindu nationalist ideology of the Indian Prime Minister Narendra Modi, whom he called a "fascist". The Muslim-majority territory is currently under heightened security, while mobile and internet services have been cut, but Khan predicted a popular backlash once such measures are lifted. "They'll come out on the streets. What happens then?" Khan told journalists at the UN general assembly. He pointed to the presence of a 900,000-strong Indian force there currently enforcing security. "I fear there will be a massacre and things will start to go out of control," the Pakistani leader said. "My main reason for coming here was to meet world leaders at the UN and speak about this. We are heading for a potential disaster of proportions that no one here realises," Khan said. "It is the only time since the Cuban crisis that two nuclear-armed countries are coming face to face.[6]

Meanwhile, Khan said he had been asked by both the US and Saudi Arabia to act as a mediator with Iran. "President Trump asked me and also Prince Mohammed bin Salman asked me to speak to the Iranians, and we are trying our best that this should not develop into a conflict," Khan said. "The good thing about President Trump is that I feel he's not a pro-war person, although I can see that there are others who are egging him on. But his instinct, quite rightly, is not for war … I think that's very admirable." In January 2015, Islamic State (ISIS) announced the formation of another terrorist group named Islamic State of Khorasan (ISKP), which represents a Salafi school of thought and allegedly receives financial assistance from secret channels across the Durand Line. The membership of this newly established terrorist group in Afghanistan and Pakistan is more than 20,000 at present, but keeping in view its sphere of influence and operations, experts fear that the group's fast growing cadre can spread across South Asia in a relatively short space of time. The Islamic State of Khorasan has recently approached extremist sectarian groups of Pakistan for support, and distributed leaflets and other propaganda material in Pashto, Urdu, and Persian languages to invite young people from different communities. This group also threatened India and Russia, and became a consecutive headache for Afghanistan. The group has established its networks in South and North Waziristan, Jalalabad, Kunar, and Nuristan province. Analyst Siddhartha Roy, (The Diplomat, 05 November 2019) has noted the threat of the emergence of the ISIS Khorasan terrorist group that has challenged authority of Indian and Pakistan governments, and recruits young fighters from both the states. The ISIS has formed another group for Kashmir as well named Ansar Ghazwat-ul-Hind (AGH) chat room:

"Essentially, South Asia is witnessing the emergence of a new brand of terrorism. Unencumbered by the strings of foreign state influence, or the weight of partisan politics and regional status quos, the new jihadists of the Islamic State era are driven by a unifying dream that transcends individual leaders. Rooted as they are in the immediate issues of local politics, building as they may be on the fertile soil of long-festering discontent and systematic persecution, they're actively connecting local issues to global ones and building a platform that goes beyond the old demarcations of territorial fiefdoms followed by older jihadist groups. Both in life as a professional jihadi and in death as a rebel martyr, Musa played by the rules of this new game: fluid allegiances and stubborn refusal to let any nation-state dictate the agenda of building the grandest state of them all — the global Islamic State — the Caliphate. A "homegrown" Indian Islamist, he was born Zakir Rashid Bhat in Noorpora in South Kashmir. He lived and studied in the state through high school. Then, like innumerable young Indian men from middle-class families, he gained admission to a private engineering college in 2011-12 — the Ram Devi Jindal College in Chandigarh. Academic straitjackets didn't suit him well. Dropping out barely a year from admission, he returned home to Kashmir and "disappeared".[7]

High profile defections in the Afghan and Pakistani Taliban increased the strength of the group, and expanded its military blanket to remote areas of Afghanistan. Police and intelligence experts in Pakistan believe the networks of Islamic State (IS) in Balochistan, Khyber Pakhtunkhwa and parts of Punjab can at any time engage with security forces. Punjab is the centre of dozens of sectarian extremist groups operating with impunity. In July 2013, the TTP spokesman told BBC that the group had established its network in Syria with the help of Arab terrorists who fought in Afghan jihad in 1980s.[8] He also admitted that 12 Pakistani Taliban with expertise in information technology had gone to Syria in 2016. In Afghanistan, close cooperation between Daesh and some disgruntled Taliban groups has added to the pain of the Unity Government. The Khorasan terrorist group, which emerged with strong military power in 2015, is in control of important districts in Jalalabad province. The group's military tactics include beheading, public prosecution, kidnapping, and torture, looting and raping, and also forcing families from their homes. Kunwar Khuldune Shahid, (Diplomat, June 18, 2019) has noted some violent aspects of the ISIS group in Afghanistan and Balochistan and argued that some ISIS affiliated groups are also active in India:

"The two provinces have been carved out of the erstwhile Islamic State of Khorasan Province (ISKP), which encompassed the Af-Pak border region. ISKP, which was founded in January 2015, months after IS had announced its so called caliphate in Iraq and Levant, spearheaded all activity in Afghanistan and Pakistan, and was the source of IS-affiliated militant activity in India as well. The two IS provinces in India and Pakistan were announced in the immediate aftermath of the group claiming responsibility for gun attacks on security forces in Shopian district of Indian-administered Kashmir. During the same week, IS claimed a similar gun attack in Mastung district of Pakistan's Balochistan province. A month before the Islamic State's creation of the Wilayah Pakistan, the group bombed the Hazarganji market in Balochistan's capital of Quetta, killing 20 people. April's Quetta bombing targeted the Shia Hazara ethnic group, which, along with the local Christian community, has been regularly targeted by the Islamic State and its affiliates, in line with the ideological goal of purging religious minorities from areas it intends to occupy. Pakistan's Hazara community has been the Islamic State's most frequent targets, thanks to an almost two century-old history of violent persecution in the region owing to their Shia identity, and easily identifiable physical features owing to their Uzbek and Turkic ancestry."[9]

Due to the weakness of Taliban and local administration, the Islamic State of Khorasan expanded its networks to all districts of Jalalabad. In Kunar, Nooristan and Jalalabad provinces, more than 13 terrorist groups are operating with their strong networks. Some of the groups including Quetta Shura, Tora Bora Jihadi group, Gul Buddin Hekmatyar group, Salafi group, Fidayee Karwan, Sia Pushan groups (identified as black-clad and masked terrorists) are in clandestine collaboration with the Khorasan group, TTP, and Lashkar-e-Islam group. In Mohmand Agency, Jamaat Al Ahrar and TTP are operating in collaboration with ISKP.

The influx of terrorist groups like Khorasan and Taliban in Jalalabad province has challenged the writ of the local administration. Afghan President Ghani also warned that 30 terrorist groups operating across the country pose serious threat to the national security of Afghanistan. The UN experts also believe that more than 45,000 terrorists are fighting against the Afghan National army and between 20 to 25 percent are foreigners. Propaganda machine of the Islamic State (IS) is also causing a great concern for parents as their school going children become victim of the so called jihadist culture. The full body of Islamic State machine is strong as its radio stations, photographic reports, and bulletins are being circulated in different languages. The Internet is also the source of propaganda of the ISKP groups where experts of the group disseminate controversial information through videos and articles. Moreover, the group has challenged the presence of US and NATO forces in Afghanistan. Last week, some members of Afghan parliament severely criticised the United States and its NATO allies for their support to the Islamic State.

They also raised the question of foreign financial support to the terrorist group, and asked the Unity Government to positively respond to the brutalities and atrocities of the IS commanders. However, Daesh has also spread its evil tentacles to the North to control provinces bordering Russia and China. The group wants to infiltrate into Chinese Muslim province and parts of Central Asia and challenge the authority of local governments there. The civilian deaths in Afghanistan have become a routine as innocent women and girls are kidnapped, raped and tortured in the group's secret prisons in Kunar and Jalalabad provinces. The Islamic State fighters are being facilitated by the corrupt commanders of the Afghan government. They are sheltered, armed and transported by them to their destination.

The emergence of Islamic State (ISIS) and its successful attacks against the Afghan security forces is considered a sign of the return of civil war to the country. Despite their drive to work together on national issues, President Ashraf Ghani and his partner Dr Abdullah were locked in an unnecessary battle for control of their war-torn country. There was a conflict amongst them regarding the appointments of defence minister, attorney general and the governor of Kabul Bank. The failure of the Afghan intelligence (NDS) to provide reliable information about the Taliban and ISIS's military strength has raised serious questions about the credibility of the intelligence mechanism of the unity government and its international partners.

One of the important functions of an intelligence agency is to provide timely warnings of hostile military action in the battlefield. Unfortunately, NDS and the army intelligence corps could not provide immediate information about IS's recent attack on the Afghan national army camp in Badakhshan province. On April 16, 2015, the governor of Balkh province accused the NDS of doing nothing to stop ISIS attacks on army posts. In an interview with Tolonews, Atta Muhammad Noor said that the National Directorate of Security (NDS) and the National Security Council (NSC) had received information two months prior to the planned attack on the attorney general's office in Mazar-e-Sharif, in which 19 people were killed, but they failed to take action.

The fate of 31 Hazara men and women kidnapped by ISIS remained uncertain. The NDS failed to determine the whereabouts of these people. President Ghani refused to deal with IS authorities regarding the fate of the illegally incarcerated Hazaras. The presence of ISIS in Afghanistan's 17 provinces is a challenge for the Afghan army and intelligence agencies. The group operates within a strong intelligence network, which cannot be intercepted by the CIA, Inter-Services Intelligence (ISI) or NDS. It has employed military experts, espionage and geospatial intelligence professionals, and executes its plans and strategies via an efficient professional mechanism. The group uses various types of encryption software in its communications. In January 2015, Afghan army commanders in Ghazni and Paktia provinces warned that terrorists associated with IS had entered eastern Afghanistan posing as refugees. They revealed that more than 800 Arab, Pakistani and Chechen fighters had established recruitment camps in Zabul and Ghazni. On April 19, 2015, Tolonews reported that Paktika Governor Abdul Karim Mateen had said that the National Security Council of Bermal district had donated $ 200,000 displaced families, which ended up in the pockets of IS fighters.

On April 12, 2015, IS forces killed more than 20 Afghan soldiers, beheaded 28 and kidnapped 10 others in Badakhshan province. Local Afghan army officials said that around 250 insurgents, including foreigners, had attacked the outpost. Some members of parliament told Tolonews that they would expose the NDS officials and military generals who had received millions of dollars from IS in Kabul. Sources in Kabul told me that the Badakhshan battalion commander had sold his military post to IS commanders. Thus, ISIS is now in control of 20 military posts in the region. Defence analyst Javed Kohistani said that more than 70 soldiers had been killed, taken captive or beheaded. He said that "the NDS was told about this a few days ago but, unfortunately, they did not pay attention to it".

Former Afghan Army Chief General Karimi blamed the commander of Shaheen Brigade, Azizullah Roufi, for criminal negligence: "Our battalion commander, without informing anyone, was in Kabul when the attack took place and now, he is under investigation." Moreover, the spokesman for the Afghan ministry of defence, Dawlat Waziri, accused local provincial officials for colluding with IS forces in Badakhshan and ultimately contributing to the massacre of Afghan troops. The police chief of Badakhshan also claimed that some local government officials, MPs and members of the provincial council had provided covert support to IS fighters. "One of the Taliban's commanders, known as Mr Abdullah, was wounded in Jurm district and was transported by a person who serves in the government," General Baba Jan told Tolonews. Now the story becomes more interesting and it is obvious from the aforementioned argument that both the Afghan and Pakistani governments and their armies do not have the authority to kill or arrest a single IS fighter within their territories.

On April 19, 2015, a member of the Afghan senate complained that in northern Afghanistan an Afghan army commander had systematically left his post and weapons to the commanders of ISIS. Since ISIS is now in control of 20 check posts in Badakhshan, there are speculations that the theft of military equipment by IS fighters, during their attack on the military headquarters, may further destabilise the region. The stolen equipment included eight ranger military vehicles, five armoured vehicles and six heavy weapons, including two DSHK heavy machine guns and two mortars. The spokesman of the Afghan defence ministry said that the Afghan army would never forgive those who killed its soldiers. On April 18, 2015, IS claimed to have carried out a deadly suicide attack in Jalalabad in which 40 people were killed and 125 injured.[10]

In light of the deteriorating security situation in the country, on April 15, 2015, Afghan lawmakers demanded the resignation of President Ashraf Ghani, Chief Executive Dr. Abdullah and Army Chief General Sher Muhammad Karimi. The interior minister and intelligence chief were summoned to parliament to explain the facts of these killings. Because the unity government failed to respond to terrorist attacks against civilians and army units across the country, the former minister of water and power, Mohammad Ismail Khan, warned that if the government does not resolve its own issues, it would face another war — this time with the notorious IS. Khan said that "if the national unity government does not reach an agreement and does not bring stability and learn to tolerate each other, this will be a critical issue to us. We fear that another war with Daesh is looming but we hope that this will not happen."[11]

A document from Pakistan's Internal Security Policy (2014-2018) categorically stated that the country's security faces the threat of nuclear terrorism. The threat, according to the document's contents, is in addition to the possibility of chemical and biological terrorism. As the fatal war against terrorism has entered a crucial phase, another powerful extremist militant group (IS) has emerged with a strong and well-trained army in Afghanistan and parts of Pakistan to establish an Islamic state. The massacre of 100 innocent civilians, including an Afghan national army soldier in the Ajristan district of Ghazni province, Afghanistan by IS forces, and the brutal killings of children in the army school in Peshawar have raised serious questions about the future of security and stability in South Asia. The Tehreek-e-Taliban Pakistan (TTP) claimed responsibility and called it a revenge attack for the Pakistan army's Operation Zarb-e-Azb in North Waziristan and FATA regions.

As Islamic State (ISIS) now controls parts of Iraq and Syria and has carried out successful attacks in Pakistan and Afghanistan, the group now wants to expand its terror networks from Afghanistan to Kashmir. According to some confirmed reports, hundreds of Pakistanis have joined the army of IS in Syria and Iraq. In October 2014, six leaders of the TTP announced their allegiance to ISIS. The ISIS propaganda material has begun to crop up in various parts of Pakistan. Secret networks of IS are in contact with different sectarian and political groups in Khyber Pakhtunkhwa province and receive financial assistance from business communities. The TTP commanders of Orakzai Agency, Kurram Agency, Khyber Agency, Peshawar and Hangu district have announced their allegiance to the IS military command.[12]

The problem of nuclear and biological terrorism deserves special attention from the governments of Pakistan and Afghanistan because the army of IS can develop a dirty bomb in which explosives can be combined with a radioactive source like those commonly used in hospitals or extractive industries. The use of this weapon might have severe health effects, causing more disruption than destruction. Political and military circles in Pakistan fear that, as IS has already seized chemical weapons in Al Muthanna, in northern Iraq, some disgruntled retired military officers or experts in nuclear explosive devices might help the Pakistan chapter of the group deploy biological and chemical weapons. A letter by the Iraqi government to the UN warned that the militant-captured chemical weapons site contains 2,500 chemical rockets filled with the nerve agent Sarin.

The most recent pattern of intense attacks by Islamic State (IS) and its Taliban allies in Afghanistan has put the credibility of the Afghan unity government and its security forces into question. IS has become a potential threat, benefiting from the changing loyalties of ethnic groups in the north and sectarian groups in the south and southwestern parts of the country. The Ghani-Abdullah government (without a cabinet) is disunited on the national counterterrorism strategy and stands at the crossroads. Both the chief executive and the president have different political priorities, which possibly caused their unsystematic approach to the ongoing, unbridled wave of terrorism. The international media recently carried stories on the presence of IS and its recruitment centres in Afghanistan and Pakistan, funded by the Taliban, sectarian groups, drug smugglers and radicalised business firms. This terrorist group also poses a bigger challenge for the Afghan and Pakistani security forces. In September 2014, more than 800 members of the IS terrorist group stormed the Ajristan district of Ghazni province, killing 100 people, including the Afghan national army soldiers.

The IS, later on, established its headquarters in Ander district where it recruits male and female Afghans for the purpose of suicide attacks. The Afghan unity government is in deep crisis and worried that this terrorist group might turn its arms on Afghanistan's weak security forces under the IS's banner. The president has already banned new appointments in the Afghan army and police department, which causes more riddles. The Afghan army is shrinking and increasingly ramshackle by the day, while the police turned to drug trafficking as police personnel have not been paid their salaries for the last six months. A police officer from Helmand told this scribe that his force has refused to defend the country without salary. The police continue to sell their arms to Taliban and criminal militias.

They are in trouble. Their children suffer starvation and are living in rented houses. This inadvisable treatment of the police and Afghan army by the unity government serves the interests of IS. Now, after the Ajristan massacre, there are speculations that IS has spread in Afghanistan and Pakistan. On November 18, the Daily Mail reported that a splinter group of Pakistan's Taliban pledged support to IS. The Jundullah group also announced its allegiance to the group. "They (IS) are our brothers, whatever plan they have we will support them," said Jundullah spokesman Marwat. In Afghanistan's Baghlan province, the police arrested six Jundullah's militants.[13]

The Daish group is also in contact with Lashkar-e-Jhangvi (LeJ) and Lashkar-e-Taiba in Punjab. On December 11, 2014, former Interior Minister of Pakistan Mr Rehman Malik told a local news channel that IS had established recruitment centres in Gujranwala and Bahawalpur districts of Punjab province. The wall-chalking campaign and leaflets prompted fears about the terrorist group making inroads in the country. According to the leaked government circular in Balochistan and Khyber Pakhtunkhwa provinces, IS recruited more than 10,000 to 12,000 fighters for the next sectarian war in Pakistan. In Kabul, on December 8, 2014, Reuters reported that a 25-year-old student from Kabul University had vowed to join the mujahideen of IS. "When hundreds of foreigners, both men and women, leave their comfortable lives and embrace Daish, then why not us?" he asked.[14]

ISIS is trying to make inroads into Afghan educational institutions to retrieve the support of students. However, on the same day, the BBC reported that the Lal Masjid's seminary had announced its allegiance to IS. On December 13, 2014, in an interview with a local television channel, the chief of the Red Mosque, Maulana Abdul Aziz, confirmed the video message of his seminary students. In November 2014, Pakistan's National Counter Terrorism Agency (NACTA) warned that IS was spreading like a viral disease across the country while the group's leader, Abu Bakkar al-Baghdadi, appointed Abdul Rahim Muslim Dost as chief of its Khurasan chapter and started gearing up to muster the support of former jihadists. Abdul Rahim Muslim Dost (an Afghan national) was arrested by Pakistani agencies in Peshawar after the 9/11 terrorist attack in the US. After his release, he wrote a book (in the Pashto language) against the brutalities and torture tactics of Pakistani agencies against detainees. No sooner was his book released by a local publisher in Peshawar that the ISI arrested him again and he disappeared for a long time. Later on, he was shifted to Guantanamo for three years.[15]

Chapter-3

Nuclearization and Military Confrontation between India, Pakistan and China

Chinese intervention in Gilgit Baltistan, and the disputed Ladakh region has definitely exacerbated the threat of war between the two states, in which the United States and European Union may possibly support India to teach China a lesson. India probably overestimated Chinese military power, while its own wounds still need treatment in Kashmir. On August 5, 2019, the Government of India revoked the special status and limited sovereignty of Kashmir under Article 370 of the Indian Constitution. It tormented the lives of eight million people. Life is paralyzed. This lockdown of 9 months and 18 days is a telling proof not only of Kashmiris but also of human rights violations. After this operation, many attempts were made by the international human rights organizations but to no avail. Media workers were barred from working on October 3, 2019. The Internet and all other services were cut off so that they could report their situation. On August 5, 2019, the Government of India revoked the special status and limited sovereignty of Kashmir under Article 370 of the Indian Constitution. Analyst and researcher Richard Purcell (28 January 2020-Global Security Review) has assessed and analysed damage of nuclear conflict between great powers:

"Nuclear damage limitation involves reducing the U.S.'s vulnerability to an adversary's nuclear weapons. It is a warfighting capability intended to enable the United States to prevail in a nuclear conflict, should one arise. There are a number of ways to achieve damage limitation, but most discussions of this topic focus on two in particular: neutralizing an adversary's nuclear missiles before they can be fired, generally known as counterforce, and intercepting incoming missiles after they have been launched but before they reach their targets. Current American policy states that damage limiting capabilities are an important component of the nation's overall strategic posture. The most recent U.S. Nuclear Posture Review, released in February 2018, asserts that if U.S. strategic forces fail to deter an enemy attack, the U.S. "will strive to end any conflict at the lowest level of damage possible and on the best achievable terms for the United States, allies, and partners. U.S. nuclear policy for decades has consistently included this objective of limiting damage if deterrence fails." It adds that "U.S. missile defense and offensive options provide the basis for significant damage limitation" in the event of a nuclear conflict. The Pentagon's Missile Defense Review, issued in January 2019, echoes this approach. It affirms that in the event of a conflict, the United States would seek "to prevent and defeat adversary missile attacks through a combination of deterrence, active and passive missile defenses, and attack operations to destroy offensive missiles prior to launch."[1]

In 2018 and 2020, President Trump and his NATO allies repeatedly criticized China for flooding global markets with cheap steel and aluminium, but China repudiated his statement. In June 2019, he raised tariffs from 10 to 25% percent on $200 billion of imports from China that were previously targeted, but some states in Asia and Europe criticized. In 2018, China also blocked Singapore-based Broadcom Limited from purchasing the US chipmaker Qualcomm. The rise of China threatens to undermine the US-led security order in Asia. Chinese military modernization, particularly in the maritime sphere, has begun to shift the regional balance of power. Analyst Marianne Schneider-Petsinger has highlighted aspects of trade war and technological competition between China and the United States:

"Moreover, President Trump signed the Foreign Investment Risk Review Modernization Act of 2018 (FIRRMA) into law, which expands the jurisdiction of CFIUS. Although this recent legislation did not mention China directly as a target of the measures, it was driven by concerns over the risks to US technological leadership stemming from foreign investment by primarily Chinese firms in American high-tech companies. One of FIRRMA's objectives is to allow for greater scrutiny of 'transactions that involve a country of special concern that has a demonstrated or declared strategic goal of acquiring a type of critical technology or critical infrastructure that would affect United States leadership in areas related to national security'. Without express reference, this nonetheless signals China is a focus of concern. In May 2018, President Trump intervened to overturn a ban imposed by the US Department of Commerce that barred the Chinese telecommunications giant ZTE from buying American technology for seven years. This came after ZTE was found not to abide by the rules of a previous settlement agreement over violations of US sanctions on Iran and North Korea. In the case of Huawei, another Chinese multinational technology company, the US Department of Justice filed a number of criminal charges against the company and its chief financial officer in January 2019, including for the alleged evasion of sanctions on Iran and the alleged theft of robotic technology. Moreover, the Trump administration has asked US allies – including Germany, Italy, and Japan – not to use the company's 5G network equipment, citing espionage concerns."[2]

The ballistic and nuclear missile competition among states in South Asia has caused consternation that these missiles can inflict huge fatalities. India's development of Ballistic Missile Defence (BMD) and number of Pakistan's missiles and warheads are ready to defeat an Indian Missile Defence System. During the last 40 years, Pakistan and India doubled the number of their nuclear warheads, making them the fastest-growing nuclear weapons states in the world. However, India has deployed a nuclear triad of bombers, missiles and a submarine capable of firing nuclear weapons. Pakistan has also developed a network of nuclear weapons factories, plutonium reactors and nuclear missiles. India has invested a lot on spy satellites, aircraft, drones and early warning radar, while Pakistan has developed spy and modern warning systems.

At present, both the states hold a massive nuclear stockpile and the size of this stockpile doubled since 1998. Both states have developed cruise missiles and are seeking nuclear submarines. China's tacit support to Pakistan for boosting the country's nuclear weapons is considered to have strategic implications for India. All these weapons and strategic developments in both states mean that confidence-building measures remain only on paper with no one wanting to extend the hand of cooperation. The main threat to Pakistan's nuclear installations might also come from a virus or worm activated within the computer. On June 9, 2014, when terrorists attacked Karachi airport and killed two military officers of the Pakistan army, the government stepped up security around nuclear installations across the country. The terrorist attack on Karachi airport showed that Pakistan's intelligence had badly failed to provide true information about terrorist networks in Karachi. This attack also highlighted the military capability of the Taliban and exposed the gap in the country's security apparatus. After this attack, Pakistanis are apprehensive about possible daring attacks against the country's nuclear installations. The terrorists yet again exposed the failure of the security agencies. This is a clear challenge for the SPD of the armed forces, which has deployed 25,000 nuclear forces around nuclear facilities.

Ravi Agrawal in his recent paper has highlighted military confrontations between China and India in Ladakh region: "In the best of times, both India and China restrict journalists from entering border areas, and the pandemic has made it more difficult to get accurate information. Let's start with what we know. This month, Foreign Policy highlighted two clashes between Indian and Chinese soldiers, on May 5 and May 9, at separate border areas in India's east and north. While no one was killed in those hand-to-hand combat skirmishes, more than 100 soldiers were injured. The Indian press, aided by trickles of information from defense officials, has since reported that Chinese army brigades comprising thousands of soldiers have crossed into Indian Territory to set up tents and trenches at key points near the Himalayas. In response, India's army has deployed reinforcements, sparking fears of a larger conflict. The Economist reports that on Wednesday, New Delhi and Beijing activated a high-level diplomatic channel to diffuse tensions. And China's ambassador to India, Sun Weidong, struck a calming tone, telling reporters, "We should never let differences overshadow our relations."[3]

India and Pakistan have applied professional measures to protect their nuclear weapons sites but nuclear proliferation still poses a grave threat to the national security of all South Asian states. Military experts and policymakers have also expressed deep concerns that if the two nuclear capable states purvey explosives to their favourite terror groups, it might cause huge destruction and casualties for the civilian populations and military installations. Recent events in Pakistan and India have raised the prospect of extremist and jihadist groups using biological, radiological and chemical attacks against military installations and critical national infrastructure in both states. The two states are vulnerable to such attacks by the Taliban and Islamic State (ISIS). Pakistani politicians are confident that the country's army is capable of preventing nuclear weapons from falling into the hands of the Taliban and IS. The fear that India and Pakistan could use nuclear weapons against each other in case of a major terror attack has not ebbed. Pakistan says it will not use nuclear weapons against its neighbours without any reason but if India were to do so, the country has the right to respond to an Indian attack.

The greatest threat to the national security of Pakistan and India stems from nuclear smuggling and terror groups operating in Punjab, Balochistan, Assam and Kashmir. Increasingly sophisticated chemical and biological weapons are accessible to organisations like ISIS, Mujahideen-e-Hind (MH), and the Taliban and their allies, which is a matter of great concern. These groups can use more sophisticated conventional weapons as well as chemical and biological agents in India and Pakistan in the near future, as they have already experimented in Iraq and Syria. They can disperse chemical, biological and radiological material as well as industrial agents via water or land to target schools, colleges, civilian and military personnel. On June 6, 2015, Pajhwok News reported that dozens of schoolgirls were targeted by unknown terrorists using biological agents in Panj Aab district of Bamyan province. This could also happen in Punjab, Balochistan, Sindh and Khyber Pakhtunkhwa or Delhi and Mumbai unless the export control regime is tightened.[4] Mir Sajad (Modern diplomacy 29 May 2020) has noted some important aspects of India-China confrontations in Ladakh. He believes that the Indian government treats people of Kashmir like slaves, and basic democratic right of exercising the political freedom too has been robbed off as more than half of political leaders are under the house arrest:

After scrapping Article 370 in August previous year China has emboldened its stand on raising the Kashmir issue twice in the United Nations joining many international countries in the unprecedented criticism of India's action in Kashmir. Before August, the last time that Kashmir Issue resonated at the UNSC forum was in 1971 and has been flagged twice since then within a span of five months. China was the main actor in highlighting the 'disputed' nature of Kashmir's historical and political entanglements. A new dimension of China's Kashmir policy has been the issuance of loose-leaf/stapled visas to Kashmiris considering entire J&K as disputed (Jayadeva Ranade, "The Age of Region: China seems to Review its Asia Strategy", The Times of India, New Delhi, 13 January 2010) Furthermore, in July 2010 China denied a visa to Indian Army General BS Jasawal (Indian Army General) on the grounds of his posting in a territory that was "head of the sensitive Northern Command based in J&K. Clarifying the denial, Beijing stated that it would not be possible to give Jasawal a visa because of his posting in the territory that was "difficult" ("Now Three Chinese Army Officers refused Visas", The Hindustan Times, New Delhi, 28 August 2010). There seems an intersection of interests in China-Pakistan relations with China investing heavily in Pakistan and seemingly 'all-weather' friendship bond between the two with Kashmir hyphenating perfectly on this mutual regional integration. In the Rambo-styled film 'Wolf Warrior 2' in 2017 China exhorted the geo-strategic message through this film by flashing the Han dynasty saying, as:"Whoever offends China will be punished, no matter how far they are". Chinese have been exhuming the ghosts of 'silk route' by announcing to the world the 'new silk route' (The Return of Marco Polo's World; War, Strategy and American Interests in the Twenty-First Century by Robert D. Kaplan, 2018) and Kashmir remain the core of that grand project".[5]

The international task force on the prevention of nuclear terrorism has warned that the "possibility of nuclear terrorism is increasing" because of a number of factors including "the conventional forms of terrorism" and the vulnerability of nuclear power and research reactors to sabotage and of weapons-usable nuclear materials to theft. Terrorists may possibly retrieve nuclear materials from India or Pakistan and use them against civilian and military installations. Another development that has also worried nuclear scientists is cyber attacks during nuclear crisis management. Cyberwarfare has the potential to attack or disrupt successful nuclear crisis management. India and Pakistan have developed strong networks of cyber armies and have often attacked each other's sensitive computers in the past. Analyst Haris Bilal Malik (Modern Diplomacy 28 May 2020) highlights the 22 years nuclearization of Pakistan and India, the danger of nuclear war and the evolving nuclear posture of India:

"May 2020 marks the 22nd anniversary of the overt nuclearization of South Asia. The evolved nuclear doctrinal postures of both India and Pakistan have been a key component of their defence and security policies. During this period; India has undergone gradual shifts in its nuclear doctrinal posture. The Indian posture as set out in the 1999 'Draft Nuclear Doctrine' (DND) was based on an assertion that India would pursue the 'No First Use' (NFU) policy. The first amendment to this posture, which came out in January 2003, was based on a review by the Indian Cabinet Committee on Security (CCS) of the nuclear doctrine. It stated that if India's armed forces or its people were attacked with chemical and biological weapons, India reserves the right to respond with nuclear weapons. This review could, therefore, be considered a contradiction to India's declared NFU policy at the doctrinal level. On the basis of this notion, it could be assumed that India has had an aspiration to drift away from its NFU policy since 2003. Subsequently, the notion of a preemptive 'splendid first strike' has been a key part of the discourse surrounding the Indian and international strategic community since the years 2016-2017. According to this, if in India's assessment, Pakistan was found to be deploying nuclear weapons, in a contingency, India would resort to such a splendid first strike. With such a doctrinal posture, India's quest for preemption against Pakistan seems to be an attempt to neutralize the deterrent value of Pakistan's nuclear capabilities. In this regard, India has been constantly advancing its nuclear weapons capabilities based on enhanced missile programs and the development of its land, sea, and air-based nuclear triad thus negating its own NFU policy".[6]

As international media focuses on the looming threat of chemical and biological terrorism in Asia and Europe ISIS is seeking nuclear weapons but retrieving these weapons from the country is not an easy task. Pakistan has established a strong nuclear force to safeguard all nuclear sites 24 hours a day with modern military technology. The crisis is going to get worse as the exponential network of ISIS and its popularity in Afghanistan creates deep security challenges for Pakistan and its Taliban allies. This group could use chemical and biological weapons once it gains footing in Afghanistan. For this reason, Pakistan is trying to push the Afghan Taliban towards a political settlement in Afghanistan to prevent IS from gaining control of the country. IS and the Taliban are not the only security challenges for Pakistan; the country is also facing many social and economic problems, including electricity shortages. Pakistan is seeking civilian nuclear technology to meet its electricity needs. For this reason, the country entered its seventh round of strategic dialogue with the US, which ended last week without any result. The US turned down Pakistan's demand of access to civilian nuclear technology and argued for focus on its non-proliferation credentials because the country always suffers from a negative image due to its tenuous nuclear non-proliferation regime.

India's policymakers are facing a strategic conundrum about how to undermine or respond to the terrorist threat emanating from Pakistan and Afghanistan. In 2002 and 2008, both Atal Bihari Vajpayee and Manmohan Singh's governments faced an unstable situation in India. The issue of the Cold Start doctrine and the possibility of an Indian abrupt nuclear attack in Pakistan have been elucidated in a recently published research paper (George PerKovich and Toby Dalton, 2015):

"Today, Indian military analysts also increasingly recognise the risk of even limited ground operation, notwithstanding initial excitement over the more finely calibrated plans proffered by proponents of the so called 'Cold Start' doctrine, similar to the ground option, with Indian forces limiting the depth of their thrust so as not to cross Pakistan's nuclear red lines. Yet, even a limited response that puts Indian boots on Pakistani soil could quickly escalate to major operations that would result in more casualties than would have been suffered in the initial terrorist attack. And, the more Indian forces were succeeding on Pakistani territory, the greater the incentive Pakistan leaders would feel to use nuclear weapons to repulse them."[7]

However, experts say that India does not have the capability to carry out a special operation inside Pakistan with precision air support. Pakistan has a strong air force and has adorned its submarines with nuclear weapons. In February 2012, the country announced that it had started work on the construction of nuclear submarines to better meet the Indian navy's nuclear threat. The current threat of nuclear, biological and chemical weapons proliferation signals trouble, particularly in the Middle East and South Asia, which will not be redressed without resolving regional conflicts, which may, in turn, require internal political changes. India and Pakistan need to implement nuclear risk reduction measures. Terrorists want to buy or steal nuclear material to fabricate a crude bomb or to make or detonate radiological weapons. Bilal Malik (Modern Diplomacy 28 May 2020) highlights the latest versions of ballistic and cruise missiles, indigenous ballistic missile defence (BMD) systems in addition to Russian made S-400, nuclear submarines, and enhanced capabilities for space weaponization:

"India's rapid augmentation of its offensive doctrinal posture vis-à-vis Pakistan is based on enhancing its strategic nuclear capabilities. Under its massive military up-gradation program, India has developed the latest versions of ballistic and cruise missiles, indigenous ballistic missile defence (BMD) systems in addition to Russian made S-400, nuclear submarines, and enhanced capabilities for space weaponization. In the same vein, India's aspiration for supersonic and hypersonic weapons is also evidence of its offensive doctrinal posture. Furthermore, India has been carrying out an extensive cruise missile development program having incredible supersonic speed along with its prospective enhanced air defence shield. Through considerable technological advancements, India has shifted its approach from a counter-value to a counter-force doctrinal posture, as it demonstrates its ambitions of achieving escalation-dominance throughout the region. These technological advancements are clear indicators that India's doctrinal posture is aimed at destabilizing the existing nuclear deterrence equilibrium in South Asia".[8]

Pakistan's 'Nasr' missile is widely regarded as a 'weapon of deterrence' aimed at denying space for a limited war imposed by India. The induction of 'multiple independent reentry vehicle' (MIRV), the development of land, air and sea-launched cruise missiles and the provision of a naval-based second-strike capability have all played a significant role in the preservation of minimum credible deterrence and the assurance of full-spectrum deterrence at the strategic, operational and tactical levels. Contrary to India's declared NFU policy, Pakistan has never made such an assertion and has deliberately maintained a policy of ambiguity concerning a nuclear first strike against India. This has been carried out to assure its security and to preserve its sovereignty by deterring India with the employment of Full Spectrum Deterrence (FSD) within the ambit of Credible Minimum Deterrence.

This posture asserts that since Pakistan's nuclear weapons are for defensive purposes in principle, they are aimed at deterring India from any and all kinds of aggression. This has been evident from recent crisis situations as well during which Pakistan's deterrent posture has prevented further escalation. Therefore, even now Pakistan is likely to keep its options open and still leave room for the possibility of carrying out a 'first strike' as a viable potential deterrent against India if any of its stated red lines are crossed.

Hence, the security dynamics of the South Asian region have changed significantly since its nuclearization in 1998. The impact of this has been substantial and irreversible on regional and extra-regional politics, the security architecture of South Asia, and the international nuclear order. As has been long evident India has held long term inspiration to become a great power. There have been continuous insinuations about the transformations in India's nuclear doctrinal posture from 'No First Use' to counterforce offensive posture. The current security architecture of South Asia revolves around this Indian behavior as a nuclear state. In contrast, Pakistan's nuclear doctrine is based solely on assuring its security, preserving its sovereignty, and deterring India by maintaining a credible deterrence posture. Based on the undeniable threats from India to its existence, Pakistan needs to further expand its doctrinal posture vis-à-vis India. This would preserve the pre-existing nuclear deterrence equilibrium and the 'balance of power in the South Asian region.

This day-to-day militarisation of potential conflict, the withdrawal of NATO and US forces from Afghanistan, and civil wars in the Middle East have all intensified the war of interests between the two states. In the presence of all these weapons, the danger of nuclear terrorism, the potential spread of nuclear materials in the black market and the recent threatened control of nuclear materials by Sunni terrorist groups (ISIS) in Iraq, has raised serious questions about the safety and security of nuclear weapons in South Asia. Pakistan faces a series of threats to its national security. These threats come from the Taliban and the likely potential use of chemical, biological, radiological and nuclear (CBRN) devices by domestic terrorist and extremist groups. The international task force on the prevention of nuclear terrorism has also warned that the "possibility of nuclear terrorism is increasing" because of a number of factors including "the conventional forms of terrorism" and the vulnerability of nuclear power and research reactors to sabotage and of weapons-usable nuclear materials to theft. Terrorists may possibly retrieve nuclear materials from India or Pakistan and use them against civilian and military installations.

Another development that has also worried nuclear scientists is cyber attacks during nuclear crisis management. Cyber warfare has the potential to attack or disrupt successful nuclear crisis management. India and Pakistan have developed strong networks of cyber armies and have often attacked each other's sensitive computers in the past.

Prospects for Cooperation on Tackling Nuclear and Radiological Terrorism in South Asia: India–Pakistan Nuclear Detection Architecture

Muhammad Umer Khan

Abstract

Terrorism has bedeviled India and Pakistan for more than three decades now. Both countries accuse each other of stoking sectarian, religious and separatist sentiments, which in turn lead to terrorist acts. India has accused Pakistan of supporting insurgents in Kashmir, Indian Punjab, and northeastern states with training and weapons.[1] Pakistan also castigates India for aiding and abetting Baloch militants[2]. Post 9/11, terrorists adopted the technique of spectacular attacks. The 2008 Mumbai attacks and the Peshawar school attack in December 2014 have affirmed credence in the fear that the terrorists will resort to any possible method to kill innocent citizens of both countries.

The geopolitical rivals have had a tortuous relationship since their respective independences, but neither of them will tolerate an incident of nuclear and radiological terrorism in South Asia. This paper will discuss the probability of nuclear and radiological terrorism in South Asia, the opportunities for collaboration between India and Pakistan to deter and detect such terrorism, and the impact of India–Pakistan collaboration.

Probability of Nuclear and Radiological Terrorism

The Federation of American Scientists (FAS) classifies nuclear and radiological terrorism in four threat categories: (1) the possibility of non-state actors acquiring an intact nuclear weapon; (2) the acquisition of enough fissile material to manufacture a bomb; (3) the acquisition of radiological material to make a radiological dispersal devise; and (4) a possible attack or sabotage of a nuclear power plant or a waste storage facility[3].

In order to gauge the likelihood of a nuclear and radiological terrorist attack, it is important to understand the ideology and motivations of the major terrorist groups in the region.

A. Ideologies and Motivations of the Major Terrorist Groups in South Asia

According to Ashley Tellis, the following types of terrorist groups operate in Pakistan: sectarian groups, Anti–India groups, Al Qaeda and its affiliates, and the Pakistani Taliban[4]. Among these groups, India specific terrorist groups, Al Qaeda, and the Pakistani Taliban are likely to employ nuclear and radiological materials to inflict human and financial loss both in India and Pakistan[5]. Osama bin Laden declared that using weapons of mass destruction is an integral part of jihad. This statement can provide inspiration to groups who share Al Qaeda's ideology to use nuclear and radiological materials in terrorist acts.

Both Al Qaeda and the Pakistani Taliban have carried out multiple terrorist attacks across Pakistan. Most notably among those attacks was on the army headquarters in December 2010, with the objective of holding senior military officers as hostages[6]. Recently, the Pakistani Taliban attacked an army managed high school and killed more than 140 students at point blank range[7]. This attack displayed that the Pakistani Taliban can resort to any tactic in their war against the Pakistani state. Such motivation has even led the Taliban to formulate plans to attack nuclear facilities[8].

In September 2012, Pakistani intelligence agencies intercepted a telephone conversation between Taliban members who were planning to strike a nuclear facility in Dera Ghazi Khan, Pakistan; the facility comprises uranium milling and mining operations, and a uranium hexafluoride conversion plant.

After the Afghan war, Pakistan created the anti-Indian jihadi network to initiate an insurgency in the Indian-held Kashmir. Gradually these groups, such as Lashkar-e-Taiba and Jaish-e-Muhammad, started attacking major Indian cities. Lashkar-e-Taiba was involved in the attack on the Indian Parliament in 2001 and also carried out the Fedayeen-style attack in Mumbai in 2008[9]. Most of these jihadi groups are motivated by the Deobandi sect, which disregards the Westphalia concept of nation states and believes in Ummah (pan-Islamism). According to Hussain Haqqani, former Pakistan Ambassador to the United States, Jaish-e-Muhammad shares the ideology of Al Qaeda, which means that only Muslims should rule Muslim land.

B. Emerging Nexus between Different Terrorist Groups

Although these groups originated to serve different purposes, a strong nexus is emerging between them. According to Don Rassler, in addition to providing expertise, Al Qaeda is playing the role of mediator and coordinator among these militant groups[10]. He further quotes Bruce Riedel that the Pakistani Taliban, Al Qaeda, and the anti-Indian militants are collaborating on terrorist attacks. Sectarian groups like Lashkar-e-Jhangvi, which target Shias, have also forged an alliance with the Taliban[11]. In 2012, the leadership of the sectarian militant groups and the Pakistani Taliban operated with impunity from North Waziristan, one of the seven lawless, tribal agencies of Pakistan[12].

Sajjan Gohel, Director for International Security for the Asia-Pacific Foundation, believes that Al Qaeda operatives were based in major cities of Pakistan and not restricted to tribal areas: Khalid Sheikh Mohammed was caught in Rawalpindi, Abu Zubaydah in Faisalabad, and Tawfiq bin Attash and Ramzi Binalshibh in Karachi.[13] Khalid Sheikh Mohammed was apprehended from the house of an activist of Jamaat-e-Islami, a major political party in

Pakistan.[14] Nigel Inkster, Director of Transnational Threats and Political Risk for the International Institute for Strategic Studies (IISS), believes that Al Qaeda has created alliances through intermarriages and business partnerships.

Al Qaeda and Islamic State in Iraq and al-Sham (ISIS) are competing for supremacy in South Asia. In order to outshine ISIS, Al Qaeda created its South Asian wing[15]. ISIS, which controls territory in Iraq and Syria, has found support among militant factions in South Asia[16]. The newly created South Asian wing of Al Qaeda launched an audacious attack on a dockyard in September 2014 to hijack a naval frigate which would have been used to attack United States and Indian naval ships in the Arabian Sea. This reflects that Al Qaeda is trying new methods of attacking western targets and it has now included India on the list of its targets.

The South Asian wing of Al Qaeda, in collaboration with Pakistani Taliban and its other affiliates, could try to procure and employ nuclear and radiological sources in terrorist attacks. After Operation Zarb-e-Azb was launched by the Pakistan Army to clear its tribal areas of the terrorist group, the risk of a spectacular attack larger than the Mumbai attack should not be ruled out. The International Atomic Energy Agency's (IAEA) Incident and Trafficking Database (ITDB) contains 2,477 incidents of nuclear and radiological material out of regulatory control from January 1993 to December 2013[17]. According to IAEA:

> Of the 2477 confirmed incidents, 424 involved unauthorized possession and related criminal activities. Incidents included in this category involved illegal possession, movement or attempts to illegally trade in or use nuclear material or radioactive sources. Sixteen incidents in this category involved high-enriched uranium (HEU) or plutonium. There were 664 incidents reported that involved the theft or loss of nuclear or other radioactive material and a total of 1337 cases involving other unauthorized activities, including the unauthorized disposal of radioactive materials or discovery of uncontrolled sources [18].

By pilfering nuclear and radiological materials, terrorists can fabricate Improvised Nuclear Devices (INDs) and Radiological Dispersal Devices (RDDs). In the past, for instance, the Japanese cult Aum Shinrikyo has tried to obtain nuclear material to carry out nuclear terrorism[19]. Experts have repeatedly said that nuclear terrorism is a possibility if terrorists acquire nuclear materials. According to Matthew Bunn, nuclear terrorism is a very genuine threat and "making a nuclear bomb is really about slamming two pieces [of highly enriched uranium] together at high speed"[20].

II. Collaboration between India and Pakistan to Tackle Nuclear and Radiological Terrorism

A. Historical Precedence of Nuclear and Counterterrorism Cooperation

There is a history of nuclear cooperation between the two nuclear-armed nations. In 1988, India and Pakistan signed an agreement, which stated "each party shall refrain from undertaking, encouraging or participating in, directly or indirectly, any action aimed at causing the destruction of, or damage to, any nuclear installation or facility in the other country" [21].

In 1999, Prime Minister Atal Bihari Vajpayee travelled to Lahore for discussions on various issues. At the end of the summit, a Memorandum of Understanding was signed, which stated:

The two sides are fully committed to undertaking national measures to reduce the risks of accidental or unauthorized use of nuclear weapons under their respective control. The two sides further undertake to notify each other immediately in the event of any accidental, unauthorized or unexplained incident that could create the risk of a fallout with adverse consequences for both sides, or an outbreak of a nuclear war between the two countries, as well as to adopt measures aimed at diminishing the possibility of such actions, or such incidents being misinterpreted by the other. The two sides shall identify/establish the appropriate communication mechanism for this purpose[22].

The two agreements are not only unparalleled in South Asia, but also provide basis for optimism that consensus can be reached to tackle the issue of nuclear and radiological terrorism. There has been precedence where India and Pakistan have agreed to work on counterterrorism in the region. In 2006, Prime Minister Manmohan Singh and President Pervez Musharraf met in Havana, Cuba, where both countries declared that they would set up a Joint Anti-Terrorism Mechanism to identify and investigate terrorist incidents[23]. Both nations, utilizing the previous agreements as a general framework, can lay out more precise arrangements described below.

III. South Asian Nuclear Detection Architecture

A. Need Analysis

India and Pakistan share a border of 3,323 kilometers. The current trade between the two countries is only a paltry three billion dollars, but with the normalization of relations, experts expect exponential growth of trade to 40 billion dollars.[24] In 2008, India and Pakistan opened a trade route across the disputed territory of Kashmir.[25] They are also planning to set up 13 border crossings in the coming years [26]. The first integrated border post was set up in 2012, which increased the number of trucks able to be viewed entering Pakistan from 150 to at least 800. This boost of trade also gives opportunities to non state actors to traffic nuclear and radiological material across the border.

In order to prevent nuclear and radiological terrorism, detection of such unaccounted-for materials is of paramount importance. Creating South Asian Nuclear Detection Architecture can surmount this challenge. According to Dr. Gowadia, Director of the United States Department of Homeland Security's (DHS) Domestic Nuclear Detection Office (DNDO), "a detection event can be in the form of information or intelligence alerts, technical detection alerts, and traditional law enforcement work".[27]

Cooperation between the intelligence agencies may not be possible because of the deep mistrust between the two countries, but a joint project of interdicting nuclear and radiological projects can be initiated by the Customs Department. With the passage of time, law enforcement and intelligence officials can also become part of the project. The South Asian Nuclear Detection Architecture can comprise the South Asian Nuclear Forensics International Technical Working Group (ITWG), jointly manned radiological detection border posts, a joint working group of legal officials holding expertise in forensic evidence, regular interaction between the regulatory bodies, and pre- and post-detonation nuclear forensics training at either Pakistan's center of excellence for nuclear security, the Nuclear Security Training Center (NSTC), or at India's, the Global Center for Nuclear Energy Partnership (GCNEP).

B. South Asian Nuclear Forensics International Technical Working Group

According to IAEA, "nuclear forensics is the analysis of intercepted illicit nuclear or radioactive material and any associated material to provide evidence for nuclear attribution. The goal of nuclear analysis is to identify forensic indicators in interdicted nuclear and radiological samples or the surrounding environment, e.g. the container or transport vehicle" [28].

A concerted effort is required to have a dedicated group of experts with the requisite capacity to perform pre- and post-detonation nuclear forensics. India and Pakistan are already participating in the activities of the Global Initiative to Counter Nuclear Terrorism (GICNT), the International Criminal Police Organization (INTERPOL), and IAEA to augment the nuclear forensics capabilities of these multilateral bodies[29]. Both countries have endorsed GICNT's Statement of Principles, which calls to "improve the ability to detect nuclear and other radioactive materials in order to prevent illicit trafficking, including cooperation in the research and development of national detection capabilities that would be interoperable"[30]. They could utilize the guidance of such multilateral forums to establish a South Asian Nuclear Forensics International Technical Working Group. As nuclear forensics requires a wide range of expertise, the nuclear forensics center should ideally accommodate legal experts, scientists, law enforcement and intelligence experts, and first responders.

The Pakistan Nuclear Regulatory Authority (PNRA) and Bhabha Atomic Research Center's (BARC) nominated officials can provide their technical expertise to the law enforcement experts from both sides in this regional forensics-working group.

C. Collaboration between Indian and Pakistani National Nuclear Forensics Libraries

According to IAEA: The State should consider establishing nuclear forensics libraries for its inventory of nuclear and other radioactive material. These libraries should include databases of all material produced, used, and stored in a State and, if applicable, supported by sample and literature archives. The State should be capable of responding to queries of other States regarding recovered nuclear or other radioactive materials that may have been produced, used, or stored on the State's territory [31].

According to David Smith, a nuclear forensics library should entail features on key nuclear fuel cycles and isotope production stages like uranium ores and ore bodies, uranium mining and milling, uranium conversion, uranium enrichment, uranium fuel fabrication, mixed oxide fuel fabrication, reactor fresh fuel assemblies, irradiated (spent) fuel, nuclear reprocessing, nuclear waste, and isotope production of both sealed and unsealed radioactive sources.[32]

A joint library between the two nuclear-armed nations would be impossible because of the sensitivities attached to the subject; however, both nations can request each other, through the point of contact, to share information if an unaccounted for nuclear or radiological material is detected. If the material does not match the samples in the national libraries, both nations can contact and share their findings with IAEA via their point of contact.

1. Verification of Data

The major problem in creating an international database is that both states have apprehensions about sharing their sensitive data.

According to a report prepared for the United States government, the major obstacles for creating a database are: commercial desires to protect sensitive data, problems related to classification and established government policies, states' refusal to cooperate, and attempts to spoof the database.[33] There can never be confidence in the South Asian nuclear security architecture if the national nuclear forensics libraries of India and Pakistan are not verified. Neither country would allow each other to verify their libraries. However, friendly countries can carry out verification. In the case of Pakistan, it can be conducted by China, while the United States can verify India's libraries.

Pakistan has always been insecure when it comes to sharing details about its nuclear program. After the United States' raid in 2011, which killed Osama Bin Laden, the then Pakistani military chief General Kiyani, feared the United States capability to launch a simultaneous attack to neutralize its nuclear weapons.[34] Due to its close historic ties with China, Pakistan considers China a reliable ally. The level of trust can be gauged by a statement of Chairman Ansar Parvez of the Pakistan Atomic Energy Commission (PAEC), who argued for a nuclear deal with China instead of the United States.[35]

China and Pakistan have been opaque regarding their nuclear cooperation agreement signed in 1986. Their cooperation started a decade before 1986 when Prime Minister Zulifqar Ali Bhutto accepted in 1976 that both countries were collaborating in this field.[36] According to T.V. Paul, the Pakistani bomb would not have existed without the help of the Chinese. They have even provided direct assistance in the building of the plutonium reactors at Khushab.[37] This shows that Pakistan trusts China and would not have issues sharing the data in their nuclear forensics library. China, in turn, could issue a quality assessment report, without sharing sensitive details, to tell the world that Pakistan has a credible nuclear forensics library.

Despite not being a member of the Nonproliferation Treaty, the United States signed a nuclear agreement with India in 2005. Under this deal, India agreed to implement the Additional

Protocol, which gives inspectors intrusive access to its civilian nuclear facilities, works towards negotiating a Fissile Material Cut-off Treaty (FMCT), and continues India's moratorium on nuclear testing[38]. Besides bringing India to the nuclear nonproliferation regime, the United States and India have formed a joint working group on counter-terrorism and signed a counter-terrorism initiative in 2010[39]. For now, this working group has mostly focused on terrorism, financial and economic fraud, narcotics, trafficking, cybercrime, and transnational organized crime[40]. The group could enlarge the scope of their cooperation to deterring nuclear terrorism and detecting nuclear trafficking. Even when India and the United States did not sign the nuclear deal, efforts were made to establish cooperation between Indian research centers and Brookhaven National Labs[41]. Lawrence Livermore National Laboratory (LLNL) is one of the prime institutions in the United States that is trying to engage other states in nuclear forensics. In addition to helping India build its national nuclear forensics library, this lab can also verify the quality of the library's data.

D. India–Pakistan Nuclear Detection Check Posts

As mentioned earlier, India and Pakistan are planning to establish 13 integrated check posts for facilitating trade. It is likely that militants in the region can jeopardize any initiative to bring peace. Therefore, these check posts must include nuclear detection equipment and trained manpower to detect illicit trafficking of nuclear and radiological materials.

Let's consider a hypothetical scenario, where a truck carrying a radiological material is interdicted at the Wagah–Attari border between India and Pakistan: the jointly manned detection post will inform its supervisors about the confiscated material. The detection post will contact both the regulatory authorities in India and Pakistan, which in turn would convene the nuclear forensics-working group. The technical experts will analyze the interdicted material and conduct a non-destructive analysis. The nuclear forensics analysis can be carried out at the post, utilizing the mobile radiological lab developed by India[42]. For a destructive analysis, the presence of scientists from both sides becomes all the more important because cooperation will result in confidence in the nuclear forensics process. The nuclear forensic analysis should be carried out as soon as possible, as it would prevent further pilferage from the source of the interdicted material.

E. Development of Radiation Detection Equipment

India has indigenously developed radiation detection equipment, which includes personal radiation detectors, aerial radiation detectors, and environmental sampling equipment[43]. It plans to deploy radiation portal monitors at all of its airports, seaports and manned border crossings by the end of 2015[44]. Pakistan, too, has a national detection architecture that covers several entry and exit points to detect and deter illicit trafficking.

Pakistan and India have closely cooperated in multilateral forums like IAEA, in the field of nuclear safety.[45] They must also cooperate bilaterally by sharing their expertise and learning from each other's experiences. BARC and the Electronic Corporation of India Limited (ECIL) of India, a subsidiary of the Department of Energy, have been at the forefront of research and development in radiation detection and environmental sampling.

PNRA has also built the School of Nuclear and Radiation Safety, which is equipped with a non-destructive lab and a radiation-testing lab[46]. Scientists from the Pakistan Institute of Nuclear Science and Technology (PINSTECH), the major research institute of PAEC, could learn from the research conducted by BARC and ECIL. Joint radiological safety training can be arranged which will help both nations improve their ability to develop nuclear and radiological detection equipment and expertise.

F. Legal Issues pertaining to Nuclear Forensics

The member states of the United Nations are bound by United Nations Security Council Resolution (UNSCR) 1540 to give nuclear security paramount importance. The resolution recognizes the grave concerns about the risk of non-state actors trying to acquire, develop, and traffic nuclear, chemical, biological, and radiological material to employ them in terrorist activities[47]. Furthermore, it shows concern that the illicit trafficking of such weapons and materials poses a threat to international peace and security[48]. It also binds states to adopt legislation to prevent trafficking of nuclear and radiological material. Nuclear forensics is part of nuclear security and cannot be compartmentalized. Therefore, an effective nuclear security framework requires stringent border controls, physical protection systems, export controls, and, most importantly, prosecution in the court of law for those who violate all such arrangements.

India and Pakistan can assemble a sub-committee of reputed jurists and legal experts within the nuclear forensics-working group to discuss the legal process for nuclear forensics findings. The legal experts can come up with suggestions for both of the legislative bodies of these countries to formulate laws that create organizations to prevent illicit trafficking. The countries can draw inspiration from the United States Nuclear Forensics and Attribution Act that was passed in 2010, which established the National Technical Nuclear Forensics Center (NTNFC) within the Department of Homeland Security's Domestic Nuclear Detection Office (DNDO)[49]. This act also exhorted the President of the United States to pursue bilateral and multilateral forums that aid in interdicting nuclear and radiological weapons and material, and investigating post-detonation scenarios involving such weapons and material[50]. Pakistan and India should also pass legislative acts that help in tackling the threat of nuclear terrorism.

IV. Impact of a South Asian Nuclear Detection Architecture

A. Responsible Nuclear Weapons State

B. Reduction in Risk of War

There is a risk of a war between the two arch rivals if non-state actors from Pakistan carry out terrorist attacks in India. Former United States ambassador to India, Robert Blackwill, believes that Prime Minister Narendra Modi would not show restraint if a terrorist strike in India is linked to Pakistan[51]. In such a scenario, initiatives like the Nuclear Detection Architecture can lessen the chances of war, particularly in the case of nuclear and radiological terrorism. The international community would also be supportive of such mechanisms since they reduce the chances of conflict between the nuclear-armed neighbors.

C. Confidence Building Measure between the Arch rivals

Active cooperation between Pakistan and India in the nuclear arena will give an impetus to the composite peace dialogue. It will be a signal to the hawks in both countries that, given the will, Pakistan and India can solve contentious issues like Kashmir, terrorism, and other territorial conflicts.

V. Conclusion

Pakistan and India have fought three wars but, as both countries are nuclear-armed, the risk of a future war needs to be minimized. In the past, non-state actors have brought both nations to the brink of war, be it the attack on parliament in December 2001 or the Mumbai 2008 attack. There is a fear that any limited conflict can lead to a "Nuclear Armageddon" in South Asia. Efforts should be made to increase the escalation ladder in the region, which has been shortened due to Pakistan's induction of tactical nuclear weapons. Pakistan has developed tactical nukes in response to India's threat of a conventional attack in case there is a terrorist attack linked to non-state actors based in Pakistan. The South Asian Nuclear Detection Architecture will aid in increasing the escalation ladder, as it will provide a platform for both nations to trace the perpetrators of any nuclear and radiological attacks in either country.

Author's Bio and Contact Information

M. Umer Khan is a graduate of the Middlebury Institute of International Studies (MIIS) at Monterey with a Master of Arts in Nonproliferation and Terrorism Studies. He received a Bachelor of Science in Computer Software Engineering from the Military College of Signals (a constituent campus of the National University of Science

Chapter 5

Command and Control of India's Nuclear Arsenal

Lauren J. Borja & M.V. Ramana

Abstract

Despite long-standing debate about the challenges of establishing command and control of India's nuclear weapons, few details about the structure and organization of such a system exist in the public domain. Objectives for effective command and control have been laid out in India's Draft Nuclear Doctrine of 1999, which was followed by the more official statement from 2003 that described some of the organizations governing the new arsenal. It is now almost twenty years later, and many changes have occurred within Indian nuclear force structure. This article documents these evolutions and details some of the similarities and differences between how nuclear weapons might be controlled in India as compared to states that developed nuclear weapons earlier. It specifically examines some of the relevant infrastructure and capabilities, such as military command centres, satellites, and delivery vehicles that have been developed in the last two decades that are important to nuclear command and control. This article also identifies continuing challenges, such as risks due to the entanglement of conventional and civilian infrastructure with nuclear systems, associated with command and control of nuclear weapons in India.

Introduction

In the roughly two decades since the nuclear weapon tests by India and Pakistan in May 1998, the two countries have had at least two direct military confrontations and one major military crisis that lasted many months. There have been reports that during these periods of heightened tensions, nuclear delivery vehicles were readied for potential use, especially during the battle over Kargil in 1999 (Chengappa 2000, 437; Riedel 2002). In February 2019, during the height of the standoff following the militant suicide bombing in Pulwama, the Indian navy deployed a number of vessels, including possibly a nuclear armed submarine (Indian Navy 2019). Mobilisation of Indian nuclear forces raises questions about who ultimately controls these weapon systems and how that control is exerted. Could they have been used by military personnel in the event of an attack from the other side, or were they tightly controlled by the political leadership?

Any answer to these questions from the outside is necessarily speculative. There is little information in the public domain on the command and control of nuclear weapons in India. In general, there has been a history of secrecy surrounding all nuclear matters in the country (Ramana 2009). Others have argued that "the level of opacity surrounding India's nuclear posture is extraordinary, and held tightly by just a handful of senior civilian officials, scientists, and officers in a dedicated Strategic Forces Command" (Narang 2013). Retired Indian military officials speak out on nuclear issues, including command and control, but separating existing capabilities from recommendations in these statements is challenging (Nagal 2014). Therefore, obtaining reliable information on the command and control of nuclear weapons is extremely difficult.

The limited literature on Indian nuclear command and control largely focuses on the institutional aspects, as opposed to the technical characteristics, and relies on interpretations of the 2003 doctrine in light of either public comment made by retired military officials in op-eds, quotes from unnamed sources in news articles on military developments, or interviews with current anonymous Indian military personnel. Analysts also often compare India's nuclear weapon developments to the historical trajectories of other nuclear weapon countries. While these are certainly important contributions, we take a different approach by examining the technical developments, such as military command centres, satellite capabilities, and nuclear delivery systems, to inform our discussion of the Indian nuclear command and control system. Instead of comparing Indian command and control to the trajectories of other nuclear weapon states (R. Kumar 2006; White 2014; Shaheen 2019), who built their systems in a different era, we discuss military communications advances, along with their potential implications for nuclear communications.

To give context, we also present a historical discussion. In this paper, we argue for the possibility that India's nuclear command and control system might have a large overlap with conventional systems. This raises the risk of entanglement and, in some cases, a greater possibility of unauthorized or accidental use. Concerns about the risk of nuclear escalation due to a conventional attack in a war between American and Chinese or Russian forces exist, because, in some cases, the same command and control infrastructure is likely to be used to direct both conventional and nuclear forces (Talmadge 2017; Acton 2018). In India, it is certainly possible that the command and control infrastructure we identify serves both a conventional and nuclear role. But less is known about potential conventional attacks from Indian enemies that would jeopardize command and control infrastructure and Indian response to attacks on such infrastructure.

Because of this uncertainty, we do not speculate further on the possibility of escalation beyond just mentioning this possibility. Even if the conventional or civilian systems are not entangled with Indian nuclear command and control capabilities, there is value in studying this infrastructure. Similar technology can be used in both nuclear and non-nuclear command centres and satellites. And the Indian defence industrial base used to construct conventional command and control systems is likely to be one and the same. We begin by discussing the differences between the older nuclear weapon states and India, followed by a brief history of the nuclear command and control debate in India. Afterwards, the paper details three kinds of technical developments that would be the most relevant for the command and control of nuclear weapons: command centres, satellite capabilities, and nuclear weapon configurations. We conclude with a very brief discussion of some potential dangers associated with the current state of nuclear command and control in India.

Similarities and Differences of Indian Command and Control to Other Countries

How Indian nuclear planners conceive and eventually construct their command and control system will have similarities to other nuclear weapon states, such as the United States and Russia. In the first decade following the development of the atomic bomb, nuclear weapon states, such as the United States and Russia, initially relied upon their existing military and civilian telephone and telegraph networks to execute the command and control of nuclear forces. The reliability (command can be expected to reach the weapon), efficiency (speed at which the command can be sent), and confidentiality (command cannot be intercepted and decoded) requirements of nuclear communications soon grew beyond the capabilities of the available networks in the 1950s and 1960s.

Additional requirements of survivability (must continue to operate, even after a nuclear detonation) and redundancy (many separate channels must be established, making it harder for an enemy to destroy all communications) were soon added. As a result, the United States and the Soviet Union developed and built separate communication channels specifically for nuclear command and control (Yarynich 2003). The emphasis on redundancy meant that nuclear weapon states deployed multiple options for sending messages to their nuclear forces, which resulted in the development of new communication technologies and infrastructure. The most outstanding example was the development of satellite communications that offered a completely different way of communicating from the older medium of ground-based radio and telephone channels. Countries also developed targeting strategies and integrated nuclear early warning systems into their nuclear command and control networks.

Alongside the development of nuclear command and control networks, modern militaries have also increased the sophistication of the command and control systems for non-nuclear military forces. Many states are expanding their military's capability for network-centric operations or the use of technology and computers to share data and information in real-time to optimize force deployment. With these developments, it is likely that some of the constraints on reliability, redundancy, and efficiency that plagued early military communications are less of a constraint to countries looking to develop nuclear command and control today.

Cyber attacks will always be a security challenge for nuclear and non-nuclear command and control, and the technical barriers to fielding these capabilities are being reduced. In addition to broad advances in military communications, civilian communications have also developed significantly since the 1950 s and 1960 s. This includes the spread of internet and fiber optic communications systems that enable many civilian sectors, such as the global financial system and social media. Some of these advancements, such as the use of open-source internet intelligence, have impacted the field of nuclear security (Bracken 2016). While these communications channels often have significant security concerns that would impede effective use for nuclear command and control, it is clear that the communications and information environment have changed significantly since the development of the first nuclear command and control networks.

Furthermore, modernization of archaic nuclear networks in nuclear weapon states has integrated information from and connections to conventional systems. Such entanglement increases the possibility of inadvertent nuclear escalation (Arbatov et al. 2017; Talmadge 2017; Acton 2018). Given that India has embarked on constructing a nuclear command and control infrastructure primarily in the last two decades, how much resemblance would it bear to the complex and, by today's standards, antiquated nuclear networks of the 1950s? The contrast between the communications environment between the mid-twentieth century and today implies that India would take a different approach towards nuclear command and control rather than simply reproduce the models provided by other states, potentially building off an existing conventional military command and control network or integrating government satellite data.

Modernization and development of nuclear delivery vehicles also impact Indian nuclear command and control development. Beyond information sharing, the skills and technologies that enable these command centres overlap with those needed to construct a national command post. For example, most Indian Air Force and Naval communications centres are capable of integrating images collected via radars, earth-observation satellites, and drones. The algorithms used to integrate and present this data are developed by the Bharat Electronics Limited (BEL), an Indian aerospace and defence company. These centres can communicate using fiber optic networks, which enable data-intensive tasks such as video conferencing, and satellite communications networks. By analyzing the reported capabilities of other Indian military command centres, we automatically collect information on potential capabilities of an Indian nuclear command centre.

History of Command and Control in India

To contextualize our discussion of the recent changes in India's nuclear command and control, we start with a little history. Even before the 1998 Indian nuclear weapon tests, early debates acknowledged the challenges of building a robust nuclear command and control system. As early as the 1960 s, when discussing whether India should acquire nuclear weapons after the first Chinese nuclear weapons test in 1962, Major General Som Dutt listed command and control systems as one of the many elements that India would need to match China (Perkovich 1999, 129). Dutt would later become the first director of the Institute for Defence Studies and Analyses, an Indian defence thinktank that frequently comments on Indian nuclear policy. His views are therefore influential. This challenge was reiterated nearly two decades later by analyst Inder Khosla: "Maintaining a nuclear deterrent requires a very high level of managerial ability.

It becomes necessary to maintain an early warning system; to indulge in wargaming nuclear scenarios; to maintain security of launchers/warheads/communications; to prevent an unauthorised launch; and to maintain a national command authority. Given the way India generally functions, is it necessary to go in for a tool so dangerous that the slightest error can be catastrophic?" (Khosla 1981).

By that time, however, those advocating the development of nuclear weapons in India professed greater optimism about the feasibility of establishing an adequate command and control system. A prominent proponent of nuclear weapons, General K. Sundarji, who later went on to become the country's Chief of the Armed Forces, argued in 1984 that "Land based [missile] systems can be more effectively and reliably tied into C3 [command, control and communications] systems, with plenty of built-in redundancy. SSBNs [nuclear powered ballistic missile submarines] on the other hand pose serious problems" (Sundarji 1984, 26). We will elaborate more on the complications created by nuclear-armed submarines in a later section.

The second major challenge identified by Indian analysts concerned a potential conflict between the civilian government and the military over the control of nuclear weapons, specifically whether the military would dominate decision-making. But this concern might have been overstated because the military had been largely excluded from decision-making in Indian nuclear weapons matters until at least 1998 and perhaps even much later. According to Gaurav Kampani, an analyst who has conducted interviews with Indian military officials, "the military was told neither of the exact number of nuclear weapons that India might have, nor how they would be employed in a nuclear war. But the civilians drew up detailed instructions to deal with problems in the absence of a formally articulated nuclear doctrine" (Kampani 1998, 15).

At the time of the May 1998 nuclear weapon tests, no new information about command and control had been offered. At an official press conference featuring the top scientific and technical leaders involved in the tests, Abdul Kalam, the scientific advisor to the Prime Minister, responded to a question by saying, "As for command and control systems, we have different forms presently, and are moving towards that" (DAE 1998). One magazine story by a knowledgeable journalist with high-level policy contacts from July 1998, just two months after the nuclear tests, reported: "it is learnt that the Government is setting up a national command post outside Delhi which would not only have all communication and radar facilities but also the strength to withstand a direct hit. Measures have also been taken to ensure proper coded security to authorise a strike.

Instead of the press of the button it is more likely to be agreed codes sent over several separate communication channels so that the armed force in charge of nuclear weapons knows it is an authentic order" (Chengappa 1998). We offer this statement to illustrate the kind of overconfidence found in Indian official statements about command and control, even though the claim about the ability to withstand a direct hit by nuclear weapon strains credibility, both in 1998 and today. The 1999 Draft Nuclear Doctrine also mentions nuclear command and control systems and included a number of stipulations. The most important of these were: "Nuclear weapons shall be tightly controlled and released for use at the highest political level.

The authority to release nuclear weapons for use resides in the person of the Prime Minister of India, or the designated successor(s); an effective and survivable command and control system with requisite flexibility and responsiveness shall be in place. An integrated operational plan, or a series of sequential plans, predicated on strategic objectives and a targeting policy shall form part of the system; For effective employment, the unity of command and control of nuclear forces including dual capable delivery systems shall be ensured; The survivability of the nuclear arsenal and effective command, control, communications, computing, intelligence and information (C4I2) systems shall be assured" (NSAB 1999). The three armed service headquarters were subsequently reported to be "drawing up detailed schemes for inducting a variety of nuclear armaments and ancillary and support equipment in their orders-of-battle . . . [and] appropriate command and control frameworks" (Karnad 2002, 108).

Although these claims about survivability are asserted in official doctrines, it is apparent that these are just a set of desirable objectives, not achieved realities in 1999 or today. Even in a state with decades of experience in deploying nuclear weapons, it is hard to believe that anything, including survivability, can really be assured. One particular assertion that we take issue with later on is the claim about tight control residing at the level of the Prime Minister; in the case of submarines, that might be at odds with the reality of trying to store nuclear weapons underwater in a delivery system that might not be confident of reliably communicating with the main command centre. Despite these inherent vulnerabilities, the Indian government continued to project confidence in its nuclear command and control structure. In 2003, when the official version of the doctrine was announced, the press release reads:

"The Cabinet Committee on Security (CCS) . . . reviewed the existing command and control structures, the state of readiness, the targeting strategy for a retaliatory attack, and operating procedures for various stages of alert and launch. The Committee expressed satisfaction with the overall preparedness" (Prime Minister's Office 2003). At the same time, India might also have received some technology from the United States, although there is no confirmation of this. In the "Next Steps in Strategic Partnership" agreement of January 2004 between the United States and India, the two countries promised to "expand cooperation" in civilian nuclear activities, civilian space programs, and high-technology trade, as well as on missile defence (Bush 2004). John Gershman and Zia Mian point out "the obvious, namely that cooperation in this context is a euphemism for the United States providing to India access to aid, information and technology in these areas" (Gershman and Mian 2005).

While speaking about this agreement, a State Department spokesman explained that the United States was ready to "help India" with command and control, early warning and missile defence and noted that "Some of these items may not be as glamorous as combat aircraft, but I think for those of you who follow defense issues you'll appreciate the significance" (AFP 2005). In a widely reported 2013 speech discussing developments in India's nuclear arsenal, Shyam Saran, a career diplomat and former chairman of the National Security Advisory Board, stated that the Indian government "has had to create a command and control infrastructure that can survive a first strike and a fully secure communication system that is reliable and hardened against radiation or electronic interference. A number of redundancies have had to be created to strengthen survivability.

In all these respects, significant progress has been achieved. To expect that these should have emerged overnight after May 1998 is a rather naïve expectation" (Saran 2013a). This suggested, first, that the process of coming up with a command and control system predated the May 1998 tests and, second, that redundancy is a feature desired by the designers of the system. Yet Saran's statement did not clarify what constituted "significant progress", leaving the details of Indian nuclear command and control developments open to speculation. The speech is important because it has been seen as being an officially sanctioned record of developments in nuclear policy. Indeed, one newspaper report described Saran's talk as "placing on record India's official nuclear posture with the full concurrence of the highest levels of nuclear policymakers in New Delhi" (Bagchi 2013).

We now turn to three sets of developments that are key to the recent evolution of command and control of nuclear weapons in India: the creation of military command centres, the expansion of satellite capabilities, and the handling of nuclear weapons. Although many of these command centres are focused on conventional military assets it is possible that some of these installations serve multiple purposes, especially considering reports that India's defence budget only covers upkeep of existing capabilities (Raghuvanshi 2020). For confirmed military bases or capabilities, this means having both a conventional and a nuclear mission. Observers of Indian nuclear forces have estimated that aircraft with both conventional and nuclear missions conduct operations from the Nal (Bikaner)

Air Force Station and the Ambala and Gorakhpur air force bases (Kristensen and Korda 2018). Satellites, too, are likely to serve both a civil and military role. As we will discuss later, analysts are divided on whether or not India's hyperspectral imaging satellite plays a primarily civilian or military role (Ramesh 2018a).

That being said, there is evidence that the military command and control structure incorporates information from civilian sources, such as data from radars at civilian airports (Pandit 2015). Due to their classified nature, only a preliminary assessment of the survivability of these capabilities is possible. Fiber optic networks can reportedly survive an above ground blast that takes out land-based communications such as telephone lines, but all land-based communications are vulnerable to local nuclear detonations on land (Fairchild Space Company 1986; J. A. Hull 1987). Historically, secure military satellites have been considered the best option for survivable command and control (Fairchild Space Company 1986), although the rise of anti-satellite weapons certainly threatens their use during wartime.

Hardened, underground command centres could survive nuclear blasts. Nuclear submarine forces have long been considered the most survivable of the three delivery options, although the land-based Very Low Frequency (VLF, sometimes referred to as Extremely Low Frequency or ELF) transmitting stations that would be necessary to send nuclear launch orders are likely to be susceptible to nuclear blast (Unnithan 2018). Reliance on civilian information and foreign hardware could also be a problem for Indian command, control, and communications. It is well documented that Indian military relies on or incorporates civilian information and data into their military networks (TNN 2008; Koithara 2012; Clary and Narang 2019). Civilian systems could fail in a crisis, which could leave the command centres operating with less information during critical times. The use of foreign components in Indian command and control centres could also be problematic. Many countries, such as the United States (T. Hull 2018), are worried that adversaries could introduce vulnerabilities into nuclear command and control infrastructure via the global supply chain.

Command Centres

India's official doctrine states that the civilian government, specifically the Prime Minister, controls the nuclear arsenal but that there are "alternate chains of command for retaliatory nuclear strikes in all eventualities" (Prime Minister's Office 2003). Hence, there must be people other than the Prime Minister who are authorized to order the use of nuclear weapons when the Prime Minister cannot do so. Additionally, members of the NCA might need to be present or in communication to give counsel to the Prime Minister (Koithara 2012). In this respect, India could be similar to other nuclear weapon states that rely on national command centres or posts to physically host or facilitate conferences to discuss and authorize nuclear plans. Information on the location and construction of an Indian National Command Post for nuclear attack planning is not publicly available. In 2004, an unnamed defence official complained that a permanent headquarters for nuclear forces had yet to be built (Pandit 2004).

In recent years, however, India has unveiled many new military command and control centres. Indian nuclear authorities at a national command centre may rely on these force-specific command and control centres for information and situational awareness, even though an explicit connection has not been made. In his 2012 book, Managing India's Nuclear Forces, retired Indian Vice Admiral Verghese Koithara asserts that some overlap is necessary between nuclear and conventional command centres, because those on the NCA will also have responsibilities in the conventional domain. He also states that a national command centre "from where the PM/NCA can control both nuclear operations and conventional operations" does not yet exist (Koithara 2012, 138–39). On the other hand, another Indian nuclear scholar, who has conducted interviews with many military officials, has argued that there is a "bifurcation of conventional and nuclear command and operations".

His discussion focused mostly on oversight of nuclear planning and the organization of the nuclear forces, not on the command and control systems (Kampani 2016). Therefore, we do not presume that India will have two separate sets of command centres. Force-Specific Command and Control Infrastructure All the three wings of India's armed forces have been building facilities for managing the command and control of weapons. Upgrades to the Indian Navy command and control infrastructure began with the inauguration of a coastal command and control centre in 2014. As the development of a nuclear-powered and nuclear-capable submarine, which will be discussed later, continues, India has also expanded its submarine communications infrastructure.

The Navy inaugurated the National Command Control Communication Intelligence (NC3I) network, an interconnected coastal command and control system capable of collecting data from various coastal radars and satellites in Gurgaon, a city just outside the capital city of Delhi (Pandit 2014c). The Indian Navy has also constructed multiple communication centres for transmitting messages in the VLF bandwidth to its submarines (Pandit 2014b; Special Correspondent 2017); some of these locations are also reported as having "elaborate communication infrastructure including modern satellite communications facilities" (Mahesh 2017). The Indian Air Force has also upgraded its command, control and communications infrastructure. In 2010, the Indian Air Force launched a secure digital network, called AFNET that is based on a national fibre-optic grid (Bhatia 2010). It has a reported data transfer speed of 500 megabits-per-second (Mbps), which is capable of supporting data intensive tasks such as voice-over-IP conferencing (IndraStra Global Editorial Team 2015).

This is also over ten times larger than the average global internet download speed of 46.25 Mbps in 2018 (NCTA- The Internet & Television Association 2018). This network forms "the backbone" for a system of command centres, called the Integrated Air Command and Control System (IACCS). The IACCS is an automated air defence system, capable of synthesizing and presenting information from various radars, satellites, mobile observation posts, airborne early warning centres, and aerial drone video (Pandit 2012a; IndraStra Global Editorial Team 2015). Some of this data is provided by civilian radars, such as those at major Indian civilian airports (Pandit 2015). These centres reportedly run on indigenously developed algorithms, which are mostly developed by the BEL company; although some sources report that hardware from international companies, like CISCO and Raytheon, was also used (Raghuvanshi 2015).

While certainly not confirmation of the company's involvement, Raytheon delivered a pitch for using its command and control systems for the IACCS control centres at the 2012 Defexpo defence conference (Bhatia 2012). New command centres continue to be added to the IACCS infrastructure (India Strategic 2018), and BEL has recently invested in a "world class laboratory . . . dedicated to the integration and testing of IACCS" ("Annual Report 2017-2018" 2018, 51). These indicate that development in the IACCS is an ongoing effort receiving much attention. Some reports also indicate that information from the IACCS can be sent to higher-level operational and national command posts (Bhatia 2012; TNN 2015). It is not clear if this is the national command post that could be used for nuclear authorization or if this is the national command post for the Indian Air Force.

The former option is plausible given the call by a prominent retired Air Force defence official for the integration of ballistic missile defence systems into the IACCS "with simultaneous dissemination of [IACCS] information in real time to the Strategic Forces Command (SFC) and National Command Post" (Kukreja 2015). Such integration, the official argues, would mean that "a fully integrated aerospace defence capability would be developed from sea level to the exosphere, against a vast multitude of targets such as the very low speed UAVs, through subsonic and supersonic range of manned aircraft, to hypersonic ballistic missiles, in a cost-effective manner". Less information is available on the command and control infrastructure of the Indian Army. As early as 2008, Army has expressed interest in underground tunnels for troop shelter, ammunitions storage, and command centres (Pandit 2008). Other sources indicated that these would be completed by 2010–2011 (Karnad 2008, 102). According to Indian news sources, preliminary work began in 2012 on seven tunnels with plans for eleven more (Pandit 2012b). The Indian Army has ordered a digital communications network from Tata Power SED and BEL that will connect deployed troops to battalion headquarters (Cohen and Dasgupta 2012; Katoch 2018). More recent reports indicate that progress has stalled on some of these plans (Pandit 2019), and some army officials are critical of its success due to delays in the fielding of the various components (Lt and General 2018).

Satellite Capabilities

India has long been interested in acquiring satellite capabilities as part of its efforts to develop a nuclear arsenal. The draft nuclear doctrine of 1999 included a call for "early warning capabilities," such as "space based and other assets" for "early warning, communications, and damage/detonation assessment" (NSAB 1999). This goal has been followed and early warning has been one of the motivations for the acquisition of various space assets (Rajagopalan and Prasad 2017, 193–212). Since 2003, Indian space imaging capabilities have increased dramatically (Clary and Narang 2019). Speaking in 2019, an Indian Air Force official remarked on this progress: "Do we need more satellites? Yes. But nearly 70% of our demand has been met and we are on track" (C. Kumar 2019a).

Since the 14 February 2019 suicide bombing that killed many Indian paramilitary police personnel, Indian officials have been more forthcoming about satellite capabilities, sometimes claiming that these satellites were used to plan and carry out the subsequent airstrikes in Balakot, Pakistan (Singh 2019a). The Cartosat constellation is a series of five optical imaging satellites with the ability to capture images with sub-meter resolution. This constellation plays a dual military and civilian government role, providing information for natural resource management and urban planning. It is possible that these satellites alone can provide images of over 80% of Pakistan's land area (C. Kumar 2019a). These capabilities, however, do not necessarily translate into constant surveillance of Pakistani territory; India's capacity for doing that is unclear.

The Indian Space Research Organization (ISRO) spent many years developing an updated Cartosat-3 (D.S. 2017). After several years of delays, the Cartosat-3 was launched on 27 November 2019 (India Today Web Desk 2019). India also operates radar-frequency earth-observation satellites. Instead of capturing visible light, radar satellites create images from radio frequencies, which can penetrate cloud cover. Examples are the Risat-2, Risat-2B, and Risat-2BR1, three X-band synthetic aperture radar satellites (Chakraborty 2018; Singh 2019b, 2019c). One other radar satellite, the Risat-1, uses a lower radio frequency (Chakraborty 2018), which provides better images in tropical climates that experience high rainfall (European Space Agency 2018).

In May 2019, the ISRO head announced plans to launch five more similar satellites within the next year (Singh 2019b). These radar-imaging satellites also perform a dual civil-military role; an unnamed source from ISRO stated that "At least four Risat satellites in space are required for security forces to keep surveillance on a particular spot on a daily basis", and images from Risat satellites have been used to conduct Indian airstrikes on Pakistani territory (Singh 2019c). In addition to radar-imaging capabilities, India also operates satellites with infrared and hyperspectral imaging. The Microsat-TD far-infrared military imaging satellite can also take images at night, though not when there are clouds covering the object being studied (Tejonmayam 2018).

The HySIS satellite can capture images across the visible, near-infrared, and shortwave infrared spectrum. While some reports have claimed it plays a military role (Singh 2018), other outside sources have pointed out that its capabilities are much more suited for agriculture and resource management (Ramesh 2018a). In addition to its fleet of imaging satellites, which tend to be for both military and civilian use, India has also recently acquired some satellites used for only military purposes. The GSAT-7 Naval communications satellite, nicknamed the "Rukmini", was launched in 2013. It is capable of sending encrypted messages over multiple frequencies (Pandit 2014a). These messages can be received by transponders in warships, submarines, and aircraft developed by the Bharat Electronics Limited (BEL) company ("Annual Report 2015-2016" 2016, 14). Launched in December 2018, the Air Force operates GSAT-7A (Rohit 2018), which connects airbases and ground radar stations, airborne early-warning and control aircraft, and drones (Airforce Technology n.d.). GSAT-7B is a forthcoming for the communications satellite for the Indian Army (Ramesh 2018b). On 1 April 2019 India launched the EMISAT, which is aimed at collecting electromagnetic signals from foreign radars, potentially helping understand their capabilities (C. Kumar 2019b).

To be sure, we cannot determine whether any of these are used for nuclear command and control. But it is plausible that at least some of these will be used. For example, imaging satellites could be used to pass on information about Pakistani nuclear capabilities or be used for border surveillance. Communications satellites could be used to direct or command conventional and nuclear forces, given that sometimes those capabilities are co-located. It is plausible that India may choose to use these for nuclear command and control, rather than develop an entirely independent system. While this cannot be confirmed, Indian military have a history of relying on civilian and, in some cases, international satellite intelligence before dedicated military spacecraft could be launched. For example, in building the IACCS network, India chose to also integrate information from civilian radar networks (Pandit 2015). Even if a separate nuclear command and control network has been constructed, we suspect that this nuclear network will integrate information from other military command and control and satellite networks. Again, we emphasize that the entanglement of nuclear and conventional capabilities could be a source of inadvertent nuclear escalation.

Nuclear Delivery Vehicles and Weapon Configurations

In recent years, there have been changes to the configurations of nuclear weapons and how they are stored relative to delivery vehicles. Historically, it is reported, the fissile cores of the nuclear warheads were kept separated from the rest of the warheads, with the former being in the custody of the Department of Atomic Energy (DAE) and the latter with the Defence Research and Development Organization (DRDO) (Kampani 2014, 99). The delivery vehicles were under the control of the armed forces.

This separation, it is believed, meant that "neither the DAE nor the DRDO nor the uniformed military would be able to launch a nuclear weapon independently, since none of the organizations – acting autonomously – would have all the necessary components to assemble a completed weapon and deliver it to target without explicit authorization from the national leadership" (Tellis 2001, 431–32).

Clearly, keeping nuclear weapons in this demated configuration reduces the pressures on the command and control system by making it less likely that there might be an accidental or unauthorized launch. But this posture might increase concerns that during conflicts, it might not be possible to bring together the different parts quickly. This concern should not exist with the most recent versions of the Agni missile. Some more recent tests of this missile are said to be from a canister (Bagla 2018). Canisterising refers to storing missiles inside a tube, called a canister, so that the missile can be protected from the elements while being transported. This makes for easier handling of the missile (Subramanian 2015). If appropriately designed, the tube can also function as the location for missile launch.

The significance of this configuration is explained by strategist Bharat Karnad: "the ongoing process of canisterising Agni missiles . . . provides the country not only with a capability for launch-on-warning but also for striking pre-emptively should reliable intelligence reveal an adversary's decision to mount a surprise attack . . . Nuclear missiles in hermetically sealed canisters are ready-to-fire weapons and signal an instantaneous retaliatory punch to strongly deter nuclear adventurism" (Karnad 2017). If quick launching is indeed the purpose, then the nuclear warheads should be mated to the missiles. We describe below the potential command and control implications of this configuration. Another indication of decreasing separation between nuclear warheads and their delivery vehicles is in the case of nuclear-armed submarines (Mian, Ramana, and Nayyar 2019). Some analysts have claimed, on the basis of interviews with military officers, that physical mating happens only in crisis situations and that "India has developed an elaborate command and control apparatus to maintain firm political control over its sea-based nuclear assets" (Joshi 2019).

However, other analysts have pointed out that even if the warheads are not loaded into the missiles, the submarine crew must have access to them while out on patrol (Sidhu 2013). And that although it is possible "to insert final components or mate a warhead in an SLBM tube while on deterrent patrol, they are complicated," meaning "the SLBM will almost surely have to be deployed in a pre-/mated state" (Narang 2013). Indian officials have used the No First Use policy to justify the acquisition of nuclear submarines: In 2009, then Defence Minister A. K. Atony stated, "Our voluntary commitment to 'no first use' nuclear weapons policy also necessitated acquiring a credible second strike capability [i.e. nuclear-armed submarines] to safeguard our national interest" (Pubby 2009). However, the constraints in nuclear-armed submarines discussed above actually make it more difficult to detect any changes in India's stated No First Use policy.

The ambiguous nature of India's No First Use policy has been previously discussed in this journal (Sundaram and Ramana 2018). We know little about of the command and control procedures for India's nuclear armed submarines. A recent description about the INS Arihant stated that "the SSBN can be ordered to launch its weapons after receiving a coded signal from India's nuclear command post", and that the Nuclear Command Authority headed by the PM could communicate with the Arihant using an Extremely Low Frequency (ELF) radio communications facility, INS Kattaboman, in Tamil Nadu (Unnithan 2018). The cause for concern is that the stealth requirements of submarines can strain nuclear command and control and increase the pressure for delegation of nuclear authority in advance. One analyst has noted that "constant communication [between the submarine and military or civilian leadership] may be undesirable, as many forms of communication make the submarine more likely to be detected" (Wueger 2016, 83).

These concerns exist for all nuclear weapon states that deploy submarines. In the United States, analyst Bruce Blair, when describing typical nuclear submarine operations, said that while on patrol submarines "observed strict radio silence" and that "no one except the crew itself knew the exact location of a missile submarine" (Blair 1985, 119). Blair has also highlighted the fact that "submarine crews . . . possessed the physical capacity to launch nuclear weapons on their own" and that under "some circumstances, the exact nature of which remain secret, a conditional grant of launch authority . . . extended to the lowest rung of the submarine command hierarchy" (Blair 1985, 101). Across all types of nuclear delivery platforms, the insertion of fissile cores into warhead and the mating of warheads into delivery vehicles makes it easier, even if not always possible, for a lower-level official to launch a nuclear weapon without authorization.

That said, officials and military officers have been quoted by researchers asserting that "highly centralized procedural control still exists over India's nuclear arsenal. Every movement, or arming of a system, is still subject to at least a two-/man rule, requiring at least two separate personnel to release a nuclear weapon, and can only be authorized directly by the NCA (i.e. an arming code with the targeting package would be communicated directly in the final step, preventing any one person from releasing a nuclear system without it)" (Narang 2013, 149). Little is known about whether nuclear weapons are kept in configurations that require personnel to use codes transmitted from central command and control centres. Because of the need for higher authentication, confidentiality, and the mobilization of elaborate plans within short timescales, other countries have developed many complicated code instructions or automated systems needed to launch weapons (Carter 1987). Even less is known about India's nuclear targeting (Clary and Narang 2019).

However, an important procedural element was discussed in Saran's 2013 speech, namely the requirement for two separate individuals in nuclear launch facilities to sign off on the use of any nuclear weapons. Saran said that the "National Command Authority works on a two-person rule for access to armaments and delivery systems" and that "Regular drills are conducted to examine possible escalatory scenarios, surprise attack scenarios and the efficiency of our response systems under the no first use limitation. Thanks to such repeated and regular drills, the level of confidence in our nuclear deterrent has been strengthened. Specialized units have also been trained and deployed for operation in a nuclearized environment" (Saran 2013a). Shortly thereafter, in a newspaper article, Saran explained that these measures are "clearly not the record of a state which regards its nuclear arsenal as having only symbolic value" (Saran 2013b).

Conclusion

In this paper, we have suggested that the "update" of the "scheme" for controlling nuclear weapons in India has evidently continued and may have metamorphosed significantly in the past ten years. A number of command and control centres associated with specific military forces have been built and a large number of satellites have been launched. Although it has not been confirmed that these command and control centres are involved in nuclear decision-making, the expertise needed to field these capabilities is similar to the expertise needed for nuclear command and control. As briefly discussed earlier, using command and control networks for both conventional and nuclear roles will expose India to new dangers, especially if they are also connected to civilian infrastructure. Even in countries that originally developed separate nuclear command and control channels, nuclear analysts have noticed an "entanglement" of nuclear and non-nuclear command, control and communication capabilities (Talmadge 2017; Arbatov et al. 2017; Acton 2018). These include early-warning satellites, radars or aircraft that perform both nuclear and non-nuclear missions.

The entanglement of nuclear and non-nuclear capabilities brings a potential increase in the risk of nuclear escalation. Because they perform multiple roles, a country looking to strike conventional communications could also threaten an opponent's nuclear network, which could result in a nuclear retaliation. In addition to increasing the risk of nuclear escalation, hackers could use connections with civilian and conventional infrastructure to access nuclear weapons systems. Cyberattacks on secret Indian government communication channels and Indian nuclear power plants have occurred (Yadav 2017; Ramana and Borja 2020). If nuclear and conventional and civil systems are interlinked, these problems might be amplified. We have also described technical developments in India's nuclear delivery vehicles, specifically land-based missiles that can be launched in new configurations and submarines carrying nuclear weapons that would have implications for the command and control of those sections of the nuclear arsenal. These developments, ironically, reinforce the perception during the early years of the debate over nuclear weapons in India, that effective command and control of nuclear weapons continues to pose a significant challenge. In particular, there remains the risk of unauthorized or accidental use.

Disclosure Statement

No potential conflict of interest was reported by the authors.

Notes on Contributors Lauren J. Borja is Stanton Nuclear Security Postdoctoral Fellow at the Center for International Security and Cooperation at Stanford University. She received her Ph.D. from the University of California, Berkeley and was previously a Simons Postdoctoral Research Fellow at the School of Public Policy and Global Affairs, University of British Columbia. M.V. Ramana is the Simons Chair in Disarmament, Global and Human Security at the Liu Institute for Global Issues in the School of Public Policy and Global Affairs, University of British Columbia and the author of The Power of Promise: Examining Nuclear Energy in India (Penguin Books, 2012) and co-editor of Prisoners of the Nuclear Dream (Orient Longman, 2003). He is a member of the International Panel on Fissile Materials and the Global Council of Abolition 2000. He is the recipient of a Guggenheim Fellowship and a Leo Szilard Award from the American Physical Society. Security and Cooperation at Stanford University. ORCID M.V. Ramana http://orcid.org/0000-0003-1332-930X

This is an open access journal. To cite this article: Lauren J. Borja & M.V. Ramana (2020) Command and Control of India's Nuclear Arsenal, Journal for Peace and Nuclear Disarmament, 3:1, 1-20, DOI: 10.1080/25751654.2020.1760021 To link to this article:

https://doi.org/10.1080/25751654.2020.1760021 © 2020 The Author(s). Published by Informa UK Limited, trading as Taylor & Francis Group on behalf of the Nagasaki University. JOURNAL FOR PEACE AND NUCLEAR DISARMAMENT 2020, VOL. 3, NO. 1, 1–20 https://doi.org/10.1080/25751654.2020.1760021-- Published online: 13 May 2020. Lauren J. Borjaa and M.V. Ramana, Center for International Security and Cooperation, Stanford University, Stanford, CA, USA; b School of Public Policy and Global Affairs, University of British Columbia, Vancouver, Canada. KEYWORDS Command and control; nuclear weapons; india; nuclear threats; unauthorized use; nuclear infrastructure and capabilities

CONTACT M.V. Ramana m.v.ramana@ubc.ca School of Public Policy & Global Affairs, University of British Columbia, 6476 NW Marine Drive, Vancouver BC V6T 1Z2 Canada *This paper was first presented at "NC3 Systems and Strategic Stability: A Global Overview Workshop" held at Stanford University on January 22 and 23, 2019. It has been revised based on comments and suggestions from the organizers and the participants at this workshop, in particular, Peter Hayes and Steve Fredkin, and then subsequently revised again based on reviews from the journal's reviewers.* *JOURNAL FOR PEACE AND NUCLEAR DISARMAMENT 2020, VOL. 3, NO. 1, 1–20 https://doi.org/10.1080/25751654.2020.1760021 © 2020 The Author(s). Published by Informa UK Limited, trading as Taylor & Francis Group on behalf of the Nagasaki University.*

Chapter 6

The Twenty Years' Crisis of Nuclear South Asia, 1998–2018: A Workshop Report

Zia Mian a, A. H. Nayyara and M. V. Ramana b

Abstract

In May 2018, the Liu Institute for Global Issues, part of the School of Public Policy and Global Affairs at the University of British Columbia, together with Princeton University's Program on Science and Global Security ran a workshop on the twenty years since the May 1998 nuclear weapons tests by India and Pakistan. The workshop addressed three broad themes central to understanding nuclear dangers in South Asia: how to understand South Asian nuclear dynamics since 1998, the present and near future of nuclear South Asia, and finally the scope for civil society-led change in nuclear South Asia.

Keywords: India; Pakistan; nuclear weapons; nuclear crisis; deterrence; peace movement

Introduction

Twenty years ago, over a period of three weeks in May 1998, India and Pakistan carried out a series of nuclear weapon tests. There were tests on 11 May and 13 May 1998 by India, one of which was claimed to be a test of a two-stage thermonuclear weapon. India's Prime Minister, Atal Bihari Vajpayee of the Hindu nationalist party Bharatiya Janata Party, which had come to power only two months earlier, later said "These tests were essential for ensuring a credible nuclear deterrent for India's national security in the foreseeable future."[1] Then on 28 May and 30 May 1998, Pakistan carried out its nuclear weapon tests. Prime Minister Nawaz Sharif of the conservative nationalist Pakistan Muslim League, who had taken office in 1997, said Pakistan "felt compelled to acquire a matching capability" and that the tests were meant to "establish nuclear deterrence" and "served the cause of peace and stability in our region."[2]

On 6 June 1998, the United Nations Security Council unanimously passed Resolution 1172, which condemned the tests and expressed deep concern at the risk of a nuclear arms race in South Asia. It called on Pakistan and India "immediately to stop their nuclear weapon development programmes, to refrain from weaponisation or from the deployment of nuclear weapons, to cease development of ballistic missiles capable of delivering nuclear weapons and any further production of misssile material for nuclear weapons, to confirm their policies not to export equipment, materials or technology that could contribute to weapons of mass destruction or missiles capable of delivering them and to undertake appropriate commitments in that regard." The Resolution also urged "India and Pakistan to exercise maximum restraint and to avoid threatening military movements, cross-border violations, or other provocations in order to prevent an aggravation of the situation."[3]

The two countries announced a moratorium on further nuclear weapon testing. There were no subsequent commitments to further limit nuclear weapon programs. There initially was widespread public support for the nuclear tests in both countries, with most political parties and much of the media in India and Pakistan largely supportive of the tests. Over time, the early public displays of enthusiasm for nuclear weapons have subsided into lacklustre commemorations and sporadic media coverage of the anniversary of the nuclear weapon tests of 1998. One official institutional shift has been the incorporation of nuclear weapons systems as national symbols in the ceremonial military parades in each country to mark on national holidays. This has gone hand in hand with the growth of aggressive nationalisms in both countries over the last two decades.

There were some public protests and the mobilization of opposition in each country to the nuclear tests, but this was largely confined to a small group of academics, anti-nuclear activists, left-wing parties and progressive civil society groups (Kothari and Mian 2003; Ramana and Reddy 2003).In Pakistan, several city-based peace groups emerged in reaction to the 1998 tests. Later in early 1999, they were brought together under the Pakistan Peace Coalition. India's national Coalition for Nuclear Disarmament and Peace (CNDP) was formed in November 2000 at a convention that brought together 115 groups many of which had responded actively to the 1998 tests. PPC and CNDP undertook educational and mobilization initiatives inside the respective country as well as in collaboration with each other. Both became much less active after a few years. The United States, the European Union and other countries imposed sanctions for carrying out the tests on both countries, including restricting funding by international development banks. These sanctions were lifted quickly. Starting in early 2000, the United States very publicly set aside concerns about India's nuclear weapons to embrace India as a new political and strategically in the effort to contain the rise of China.

The United States responded to the attacks of 11 September 2001 by prioritizing its need for Pakistan's support for the war in Afghanistan over concerns both about Pakistan's nuclear weapons activities and the military coup of October 1999 that overthrew Nawaz Sharif and brought General Musharraf to power. In the wake of the nuclear tests came nuclear crises. India and Pakistan went to war between May and July 1999 after Pakistan sent forces across the Line of Control into the Kargil region of India-held Kashmir. The war ended with Pakistan feeling compelled to withdrew its forces in Kargil as they faced defeat and international concern about the possible escalation of the conflict to nuclear war.

Then, following an attack on India's Parliament on 13 December 2001, there was a major 14 month long military crisis in 2001–2002, with large-scale deployments along the border, which led many to expect war. No military crisis as severe as these has emerged since then between the two states despite events that could in principle have led to escalation. Most notably, India was restrained in its response to the 2008 attacks on Mumbai which killed almost 200 people by Islamist militant's affliated with the Lashkar-e-Taiba, a Pakistani group with ties to the state. Meanwhile, throughout the past two decades, India and Pakistan have been working on building up their nuclear arsenals, but have carried out no further nuclear weapon tests. It has been estimated that India's stockpile has grown from about 3 weapons in 1998 to 140 weapons as of 2018 (Kristensen and Norris 2013; Kristensen and Norris 2018).

In this same twenty-year period, Pakistan's arsenal is estimated to have grown from about 2 weapons to 150 weapons, as of 2018. Both countries now appear to have developed nuclear weapons that can be delivered by a triad: by aircraft, by land-based missiles, and from submarines at sea, although some of these capabilities are still being tested. India and Pakistan also have built up their infrastructure for producing plutonium and highly enriched uranium – the key ingredients for nuclear weapons. Finally, both countries have put in place military, technical and political institutional structures and operating principles and financial resources for managing the growth and possible use of their arsenals.

Workshop Description

The one and half day workshop covered three major themes. The first theme involved understanding South Asian nuclear dynamics since 1998. This focused on the related questions of whether developments in the nuclear complexes in India and Pakistan since 1998 had been as expected with regards to weapons systems, weapons capabilities, missile material production, nuclear postures and policies, and to what extent there had been unexpected developments. The discussion also focused on whether there were signs of what could be interpreted as processes of nuclear learning or innovation as opposed to mimetic processes in which India and Pakistan selected from and copied existing types of nuclear weapons systems, capabilities, postures and policies associated with other nuclear weapon states at various stages of their development.

The final topic discussed was whether there had been any major nuclear crises since those of 1999 and 2001–2002 and, if none, to what extent this could be seen as the result of a "nuclear crisis ratchet effect" where the experience of nuclear crises affected subsequent behaviour by inducing caution or fuelling confidence about crisis behaviour and outcomes. The second major theme of the workshop was the present and near future of nuclear South Asia. The questions here related to assessing the current nuclear situation, identifying key drivers and what could be expected looking forward, including whether the present dynamics are expected to persist, slow down, stop, or go into reverse. The third and final broad theme of the workshop concerned the scope for interventions, civil society agency and change in nuclear South Asia.

The main focus was the experience of the past 20 years with regard to civil society and democratic processes in shaping nuclear debates and nuclear policies in India and Pakistan. This included an assessment of what has worked and what has not worked so far in the efforts by anti nuclear movements in South Asia. A final concern was whether anti-nuclear groups had resources or prospective windows of opportunity to try something new or different or whether it required waiting for circumstances to change. The discussion during the workshop is briefly summarised below and organized around four broad sets of issues.

Divergent Expectations and Understandings

One major debate among participants concerned the question of whether it was possible to uniquely specify a set of expectations about what India and Pakistan would do after the May 1998 tests, prior to those events. Some participants felt that the two countries were expected to follow the Cold War trajectory. This meant that although India and Pakistan were officially making statements about only having a capability for minimum deterrence, both were expected to build a large number of weapons and expand the race. Others were surprised at the on-going expansion because the political science and strategic literature in the 1990s predicted that India and Pakistan would adopt a different approach from the traditional nuclear weapon states with a relatively limited arsenal. Those in the latter camp have been surprised by, for example, the two countries desiring to build a triad of delivery vehicles.

Those in the former group attribute the statements about only desiring a minimal nuclear arsenal to technical constraints: limited availability of missile materials (plutonium and highly enriched uranium) and only a limited number of potential delivery vehicles. A second debate was concerned with Pakistan's ability to make nuclear weapons, which has implications for thinking about other countries acquiring nuclear weapons in the future. Some thought that Pakistani scientific manpower was inadequate and the only way the country could have produced nuclear weapons was because it received substantial help from China. Others felt that China's role may have served to only accelerate the development of Pakistan's nuclear weapons and were not a decisive factor.

This was because making nuclear weapons is no longer as challenging as it may have been in the 1950s and 1960s, and since then it has been possible for proliferant states to acquire much of the necessary missile material production and missile technology from other countries. Regardless of the debate of what should have been expected of the two countries in 1998, today both countries are seen to be following an open-ended arms race of the kind that characterized the Cold war albeit on a much smaller scale.

Nuclear Drivers: Technology, Policy and Institutions

Another set of discussions during the workshop concerned the drivers for nuclear developments in India and Pakistan. Three possible contenders are technological momentum, policy choices made by national leaders and political parties, and institutional interests. If the first factor is the dominant driver, then India and Pakistan would essentially develop all the different kinds of weapons and delivery vehicles they are capable of developing and the arsenal would keep on growing in size and sophistication. The importance of the second factor was apparent in India's weapons tests of May 1998, which was decided by the Bharatiya Janata Party that had come to power a few weeks earlier.

Finally, bureaucratic and institutional interests determine various aspects of the nuclear arsenal, such as the relative importance given to the different arms of the triad, the division of control between the civilian leadership and the military, and the pursuit of policies and resources to create additional and new weapon systems, capabilities and facilities on the part of the nuclear weapons research, development and production complex. Both countries have seen the rise of a new set of nuclear policy focused think tanks and academic programs that increasingly dominate the public narrative on nuclear weapons policy. They tend to advocate a belligerent, expansive nuclear arsenal and postures, based on conservative readings of classic Cold War American nuclear strategic texts, and oppose disarmament and arms control measures.

The relative importance of these three different factors was debated, although it was recognized that the importance varied between India and Pakistan. But depending on the relative importance, one can envision different futures. For example, if technological development is the primary driver, then doctrine or policies will not affect the trajectory.

From the Outside in: The Changing Global Context of Nuclear South Asia

What happens in India and Pakistan is strongly shaped by two powerful countries outside the region: China and the United States of America. The debate over the role of China in shaping Pakistan's nuclear arsenal has already been described. But looking to the future, some suggested that the architecture of the Chinese arsenal, which is very different from the US triad, might have an impact on how Pakistan's nuclear arsenal evolves. However, others pointed out that China's nuclear postures were themselves evolving, and the country was modernizing its arsenal. Earlier economic development was the priority for China's leadership, and nuclear weapons were sidelined, but in the past two decades, a larger and rapidly growing economy has allowed a major commitment to modernization of China's military and nuclear weapons capabilities. Others pointed out that after the Kargil war, the dynamic had changed, leading to, for example, Pakistan's development of tactical nuclear weapons.

The role of China in South Asia is also changing, especially since Xi Jinping came to power and started initiatives like One Belt One Road. As a result, China has been responsible for large capital flows into Pakistan. In comparison, although the Indian and Chinese economies are getting more integrated, that is seen as a problem in India because of its growing trade deficit and dependence on Chinese products. The role of the United States has changed a lot since the attacks of 11 September 2001, which had a huge impact on South Asian politics. In Pakistan, especially, General Pervez Musharraf was forced to join the United States in some of its actions in Afghanistan, which led to significant domestic strife and concern about the possibility of nuclear weapons reaching the hands of terrorists.

On the Indian side, the major development came with the US-India nuclear deal that demonstrated that the two countries were entering into a new level of strategic relationship. Although clearly in relative decline compared to its power and influence at the end of the Cold War and the decade that followed, the United States still shapes the discussion and the framework of South Asian security and will continue to be involved in South and East Asia unless an Asian security system is established. The relationship between these two countries, the United States and China, is itself evolving, including in the military dimension. India and Pakistan will have to adjust to these changes and fit into US and Chinese policy rather than expect to drive these policies.

From the Ground up: Civil Society, Media and Democracy

Both India and Pakistan have seen the growth of peace movements in the aftermath of the nuclear tests. But these have not managed to change policy in any significant way. They operate more as irritants, reminding the public about the dangers and costs of nuclear weapons development and trying to delegitimize the governments in their efforts. In both countries, there have been significant challenges. In India, the character of middle class, which is somewhat different from Western nuclear states, has been a limiting factor in the effectiveness of the peace movement. In Pakistan, the peace movement faced a very strong, at times harsh, reaction from the state, mostly in the form of harassment and personal intimidation, as well as from the public. Peace groups have found it hard to gain access to a media that has become less interested in covering nuclear policy, except during crisis, and is anyway increasingly fragmented and losing its audience to social media.

The traditional print news media has ceased to offer a critical independent voice, in part because of changing business models, which has contributed to a normalization of nuclear weapons in both countries. In both countries, there has been greater involvement by a larger set of people when there were struggles against nuclear power plants and other facilities at specific locations. In India, the struggle against the Koodankulam nuclear plant that was constructed by Russia is well known. In Pakistan, there was some mobilization against the nuclear power plants being built by China in Karachi and there was even a legal case that resulted in a temporary stay order against the construction of the plant, but it was later removed. The power plants have now been brought under the China-Pakistan Economic Corridor (CPEC), which makes it harder to resist.

Acknowledgements

The workshop involved scholars from Canada, India, Pakistan, the United Kingdom, and the United States. The participants were Pervez Hoodbhoy (currently Zohra and Z.Z. Ahmad Distinguished Professor of Physics and Mathematics at Forman Christian College-University, Lahore), A.H. Nayyar (retired Professor of Physics from the Department of Physics, Quaide-Azam University, Islamabad) and Sadia Tasleem (Department of Defence and Strategic Studies, Quaid-e-Azam University, Islamabad) from Pakistan; Achin Vanaik (retired Professor of International Relations and Global Politics, University of Delhi, and Coalition for Nuclear Disarmament and Peace) and C. Rammanohar Reddy (former Editor of Economic and Political Weekly) from India; Raminder Kaur (Professor of Anthropology & Cultural Studies at the University of Sussex) from the United Kingdom; Zia Mian (co-director of the Program on Science and Global Security, Princeton University), Shampa Biswas (Paul Garrett Professor of Political Science, Whitman College), Karthika Sasikumar (Associate Professor of Political Science, San Jose State University), Gaurav Kampani (Assistant Professor of Political Science at the University of Tulsa in Oklahoma) and Bharath Gopalaswamy (Director of the South Asia Center, Atlantic Council, Washington DC) from the United States; and Robert Anderson (Professor of Communication, Simon Fraser University) and M.V. Ramana (Professor and Simons Chair in Disarmament, Global and Human Security at the School of Public Policy and Global Affairs, University of British Columbia) from Canada. All discussions at the workshop were on a strict not-for-attribution basis. However, some of the presentations at the workshop are being written up and will be published in a future issue of this journal.

Disclosure Statement; No potential conflict of interest was reported by the authors.

Notes on Contributors

Zia Mian is co-director of the Princeton University's Program on Science and Global Security, which is part of the Woodrow Wilson School of Public and International Affairs. He also directs the Project on Peace and Security on South Asia. He is co-author with Harold Feiveson, Alexander Glaser, and Frank von Hippel of "Unmaking the Bomb: A Fissile Material Approach to Nuclear Disarmament and Nonproliferation" (MIT Press, 2014). A. H. Nayyar is a visiting researcher at the Princeton University's Program on Science and Global Security, which is part of the Woodrow Wilson School of Public and International Affairs. He works with the Project on Peace and Security on South Asia. He has taught in the Department of Physics, Quaid-i-Azam University Islamabad and was Visiting Professor of Physics, Lahore University of Management Science Lahore. M. V. Ramana is the Simons Chair in Disarmament, Global and Human Security at the Liu Institute for Global Issues in the School of Public Policy and Global Affairs, University of British Columbia and the author of The Power of Promise: Examining Nuclear Energy in India (Penguin Books, 2012) and co-editor of Prisoners of the Nuclear Dream (Orient Longman, 2003). Physical Society.ORCID Zia Mian http://orcid.org/0000-0002-0802-2306 M. V. Ramana http://orcid.org/0000-0003-1332-930X. The Twenty Years' Crisis of Nuclear South Asia, 1998–2018: A Workshop Report, Zia Mian, A. H. Nayyar & M. V. Ramana. To cite this article: Zia Mian, A. H. Nayyar & M. V. Ramana (2018) The Twenty Years' Crisis of Nuclear South Asia, 1998–2018: A Workshop Report, Journal for Peace and Nuclear Disarmament, 1:2, 529-535, DOI: 10.1080/25751654.2018.1527807. To link to this article: https:// doi.org/10.1080/25751654.2018.1527807. © 2018 The Author(s). Published by Informa UK Limited, trading as Taylor & Francis Group on behalf of the Nagasaki University. © 2018 The Author(s). Published by Informa UK Limited, trading as Taylor & Francis Group on behalf of the Nagasaki University. This is an Open Access article distributed under the terms of the Creative Commons Attribution License (http://creativecommons.org/ licenses/by/4.0/), which permits unrestricted use, distribution, and reproduction in any medium, provided the original work is properly cited.

Chapter 7

India-Pakistan Crises under the Nuclear Shadow: The Role of Reassurance

Karthika Sasikumar

Abstract

This paper will examine four crises that took place between India and Pakistan, in the period in which they were declared nuclear powers. It shows that by combining threats and reassurance, Indian leaders sought to avert nuclear use, while deriving strategic and diplomatic gains from the presence of nuclear weapons. While scholars differ as to whether India-Pakistan crises should be termed "nuclear crises", this paper asks instead how one state –India–behaves during crises, simultaneously drawing attention to, and downplaying its nuclear dimensions. The first section of the paper explains the role of reassurance in the complex game of deterrence. The second section provides a brief summary of the India-Pakistan nuclear relationship. The four crises are analyzed in the third section. Each crisis is first summarized, and the words and deeds that New Delhi chose to signal reassurance are highlighted. The fourth and final section evaluates whether the nuclear danger can be thus managed through the calibration of threat and reassurance. It identifies three factors that impede signals of reassurance, and cautions that the balance between threat and reassurance is too delicate to be relied on to keep the peace between India and Pakistan.

Keywords: India; nuclear; deterrence; Pakistan; media

Introduction

The relationship between India and Pakistan is characterized by intense crises at irregular intervals. Since the late 1980s, there has been a risk that any serious crisis could terminate in a nuclear exchange. Scholars have examined the probability, and the potential costs of, such an exchange. They have focused on the threats issued, before and during the crises. They have examined the roles of the United States and other major powers in the crises. The main debate has centered on whether nuclear weapons caused crises, or whether they helped resolve crises between India and Pakistan. In fact, nuclear optimists and nuclear pessimists differ on what a nuclear crisis is. Consequently, it is difficult to answer the question:

"Why have there been no nuclear crises between India and Pakistan?" This paper instead asks a different question: how one state – India – behaves during crises. It finds that although analyses of crises are more likely to discuss signals of threat, signals of reassurance during crises are vital to avoiding a nuclear exchange. At the same time, it also finds three factors that impede signals of reassurance, and cautions that the balance between threat and reassurance may be too delicate to keep the peace between India and Pakistan. This paper will examine four crises that took place between India and Pakistan after the formal declaration of nuclear possession by the two countries in 1998. While threats are readily perceived, the role of reassurance in these crises has been somewhat neglected.

The paper reveals the ways in which India has reassured Pakistan. By reassurance, I mean actions and statements by political and military leaders intended to signal that the country's response is rational, motivated by strategic – rather than partisan – objectives, and limited in time and geographic scope. Most importantly, Indian signals heighten the adversary's assumption that nuclear weapons will not be used. All four crises had the potential to escalate to the level of nuclear use. They fit the definition of nuclear crisis advanced by Richard Betts: a crisis including "any official suggestion that nuclear weapons may be used". These official suggestions are of two types. The first type includes declarations or hints, through public statements, diplomatic channels, or deliberate leaks.

The second type includes actions such as observable preparations, and the exercising of nuclear capabilities beyond normal peacetime status (Betts 1987, 6). The first section of the paper explains the role of reassurance in the complex game of deterrence. The second section provides a brief summary of the India-Pakistan nuclear relationship. The four crises are analyzed in the third section. Each crisis is first summarized, and the words and deeds that New Delhi chose to signal reassurance are highlighted. The fourth and final section evaluates whether the nuclear danger can be thus managed, through the calibration of threat and reassurance.

Reassurance: Its Role in Deterrence

When crises occur between two states that possess nuclear weapons, nuclear pessimists focus on causation, on the role of nuclear weapons in facilitating or igniting crises. For example, Pervez Hoodbhoy describes the Kargil conflict as the first war that was caused by nuclear weapons (Hoodbhoy 2013, 73). Paul Kapur presents Kargil as evidence of Pakistani leaders' faith in the "insulating effects" of nuclear weapons. He writes: "After the 1998 Indo-Pakistan nuclear tests, Pakistani leaders believed that their overt nuclear capacity would provide them with more robust deterrence than their earlier undeclared capability had done" (Kapur 2006, 40). While Kapur terms this process nuclear "emboldenment", Asad Durrani, former Director-General of Pakistan's Inter Services Intelligence, describes it as a belief in "nuclear immunity" (Dulat, Durrani, and Sinha 2018, 134).

Nuclear pessimists hold organizational problems (inherent to nuclear arsenals) and political structures (specific to countries) responsible for crises. Scott Sagan, for example, points out that military biases towards fast and pre-emptive action are magnified in a polity such as Pakistan, which has weak civilian control of the military and inadequate technical safeguards against unauthorized use (Sagan and Waltz 2003). While pessimists focus on the causal link between nuclear weapons and crises, nuclear optimists focus on crisis resolution. They point out that a nuclear exchange has not yet occurred in South Asia, and give the credit to deterrence (Hagerty 2008; Sagan and Waltz 2003). For example, Rajesh Rajagopalan claims that India's fear of nuclear escalation was the main factor in its restraint during the Kargil crisis, which ultimately led to its resolution (Rajagopalan 2008).

Nuclear optimists attribute crises to domestic political causes. For example, civil-military dynamics and misperceptions within Pakistan, rather than nuclear acquisition, are said to have motivated the Pakistani military to occupy the Kargil heights in 1999 (Lavoy 2009; Pegahi 2018). Mark Bell and Julia Macdonald argue that there is no scholarly consensus on the likelihood of nuclear use – and therefore on the question of whether nuclear weapons prevent or aggravate conflict – because different nuclear crises operate according to different logics (Bell and Macdonald 2019). Focusing on the causes and resolution of crises obscures the events that take place during the crisis. This paper turns its attention to the processes under way as a crisis progresses, rather than engage in the debate on the role of nuclear weapons in triggering conflict.

It investigates the methods by which India seeks to ensure that crises are terminated with minimal risk of a nuclear exchange, while also extracting the maximum geopolitical benefit for itself. These methods include both threat and reassurance. Nuclear deterrence depends on the credibility of a state's retaliation. Credibility, in turn, rests on both capability and intention. While capability refers to nuclear weapons hardware and their command and control systems, intention is a complex psychological phenomenon. The government must signal that it is able and willing to respond to certain threats (but not others) with nuclear weapon use. Thus, intention has two components that seem at first glance to be at cross-purposes. First, intention must convey threat. The government must convince the adversary that it will carry out a nuclear strike if so-called "red lines" are crossed. Second, signals of intention must also reassure: that unless and until those lines are crossed, nuclear weapons will be kept in reserve, and used only as a deterrent. They will not be brandished in minor crises, in anger or vengeance, or deployed for partisan political purposes.

Why is reassurance important for deterrence? Firstly, if messaging consisted only of threats, the adversary would have little incentive to stay its hand. If Pakistan believed that India was capable of launching a full-scale attack (potentially including a nuclear strike) at the slightest provocation, it would make sense to launch a Pakistani strike first. This would make deterrence dangerously unstable. Deterrence requires all parties involved to maintain the right balance between threat and reassurance. Secondly, parties other than the adversary also need to be reassured. In general, the international norm of nuclear non-use privileges deterrence as a last resort, and frowns on attempts at nuclear compellence. As Matthew Fuhrmann and Todd Sechser put it, a state that attempted overt compellence would ". . . provoke an international backlash, potentially triggering economic sanctions and international isolation, encouraging nuclear proliferation, and provoking other states to align against it" (Fuhrmann and Sechser 2013, 177).

India is eager to brand itself as a responsible holder of nuclear weapons, and therefore is particularly concerned with portraying its nuclear arsenal as a pure deterrent. How is reassurance conveyed to the adversary? Reassuring signals include both declaratory statements and actions on the ground. Statements are made by elected leaders or military authorities. At times, important individuals outside the chain of command can also make these statements. Actions include troop deployments and withdrawals, visible changes in alert status, the movement of conventional and nuclear weapons, and actual kinetic operations carried out by troops. The existence of democratic institutions can contribute to reassurance. Although the 1998 tests were condemned by all major powers, as well as the bulk of membership of the United Nations, the world eventually came to accept India's possession of nuclear weapons. This can be seen in the 2005 description of India as a "responsible state" in the India-United States joint statement, which was seen as a recognition of India as a de facto Nuclear Weapon State.

India is even being considered for membership of the Nuclear Suppliers Group. This acceptance has come about partly as a result of the emphasis that India placed on the strength of its democracy and civilian control of nuclear assets (Hayes 2009; Sasikumar 2007). However, certain features of India's democracy could weaken reassurance: the need for political parties to appear strong and decisive (especially around elections); the rising salience of security issues among the attentive public; and the growth of Hindu majority nationalism, which leads to tension with the Muslim minority, and with Pakistan. "Reassurance" is used in the security studies literature to describe actions that states take to reduce their adversaries' apprehension of being attacked. Evan Braden Montgomery, writing about the security dilemma in general, defines reassurance as the actions taken by a "benign state" to reveal its motives to its adversaries, "by taking actions that decrease its ability to defeat them in the event of a conflict" (Montgomery 2006, 151).

In this paper, it is not assumed that India is a benign power, which is trying to signal that Pakistan is not a target. The paper makes no assumptions about Indian motivations, other than the desire to avoid nuclear war. Michael Howard uses the term "reassurance" as distinct from nuclear deterrence, possibly even opposed to it. He describes the presence of US conventional forces in Europe during the Cold War as providing reassurance to the European allies (Howard 1982–1983). In this paper, reassurance strategies are targeting not Indian citizens or allies, but decision-makers in Pakistan. In the literature on nuclear weapons, reassurance has a more specific meaning. For instance, Janne Nolan states that reassurance was the goal of the US nuclear policy under the Carter administration – in contrast to earlier policies that emphasized launch on warning (Nolan 2000, 13).

Here, it is clear that reassurance aims merely to prevent the adversary (the Soviet Union) from over-reacting. Reassurance and restraint are sometimes used as synonyms. In this paper, reassurance refers to a type of crisis behavior, which manifests itself once a crisis is under way. Restraint is a broader, more general strategy. India's response to the 2006 bombing is an example of restraint. In July 2006, a series of crude bombs went off on packed local trains in India's commercial hub, Mumbai, killing over two hundred people. The finger of suspicion pointed immediately to Lashkar-e-Taiba – a group historically supported by the Pakistani state. In the aftermath of the bombing, India suspended talks with Pakistan, but resisted pressure to take military action (Anon 2006). In 2013, two soldiers were attacked on the Line of Control (LoC), the de facto border between India and Pakistan. Again, the government eschewed a military response, in spite of stringent calls to action from opposition parties (Sharma 2013). Reassurance can also be conceptually distinguished from de-escalation. Reassurance, for the purposes of this analysis, refers to signals that nuclear weapons will not be used. De-escalation refers to any move during a crisis, referring to conventional, nuclear, and even non-military sparring, that indicates a desire to lower tensions. Thus, reassurance is a subset of de-escalation. However, in practice, conventional de-escalation during a crisis can be a signal of nuclear reassurance. An example, discussed below, was India's choice to restrict conventional military operations during the Kargil War.

The India–Pakistan Deterrence Relationship

The three main factors at play in the strategic relationship between India and Pakistan are nuclear weapons, terrorism, and the concerns of the international community – specifically the United States. In May 1998, India and Pakistan tested nuclear devices and declared themselves as Nuclear Weapon States. However, both countries possessed the ability to deliver nuclear weapons on each other's territory since the late 1980s. The 1998 tests caused great concern in the international community, because the two countries have several intense and unresolved conflicts, and share a contested border. Crises between India and Pakistan continued to occur after 1998, attracting the concern of scholars and policy-makers.

These crises have been explained by the stability-instability paradox. This concept recognizes that while the possibility of fullscale war is eliminated by the desire to avoid a nuclear exchange, there are strong incentives for sub-strategic operations (e.g. sponsoring militant attacks and launching limited military operations). In fact, the more credible deterrence becomes at the strategic level, the more violence we would expect at the sub-strategic level (Ganguly 1995; Tellis 1997). These violent operations would be carried out by the revisionist power – in this case, Pakistan – banking on the deterrent power of its nuclear arsenal. Paul Kapur proposes an explanation that is an alternative to the stability-instability paradox.

In his account, Pakistani leaders bet that although India could use its conventional superiority to reverse Pakistani territorial gains, it will refrain for fear of a nuclear attack. It is not stability but instability, "the danger of nuclear escalation, that allows weak, revisionist Pakistan to undertake limited conventional aggression against India in hopes of altering regional boundaries without provoking a full-scale Indian conventional response" (Kapur 2006, 41). In fact, both those who posit the relevance of the paradox, and those who claim that conflict between India and Pakistan is not due to the paradox, assume that Pakistan is revisionist. Both assume that India has strong incentives to refrain from nuclear use. If it were thought that India would run any risk – including suffering a nuclear attack – in order to protect its territorial integrity, Pakistan would not be emboldened.

This paper focuses on India's incentives, and examines why and how India signals that nuclear weapons will not be used. Another crucial factor in the India-Pakistan situation is cross-border terrorism. Several militant outfits operating out of Pakistan have vowed to carry out attacks on Indian soil. The extent to which these groups are supported by the Pakistani state (or certain elements of that state) is a matter of heated debate. Nevertheless, when there are terrorist attacks on Indian assets, the involvement of the Pakistani government is immediately assumed in Indian public opinion. Consequently, the democratically elected government in New Delhi feels impelled to respond to the (supposed) provocation by Islamabad. The international community, and in particular the United States, are concerned about India-Pakistan interactions.

This concern is the third significant factor in the deterrence relationship. During a crisis, India must reassure the international community that it is neither contemplating nor provoking the use of nuclear weapons. How has India responded to these three factors? To be sure, several Indian leaders have affirmed over two decades that nuclear deterrence is in operation in South Asia, and that the option of a full-scale war is off the table (Anon 2016b; Thapar 2008). India has made a formal declaration of No First Use (NFU), stating that it will not use nuclear weapons first, only in response to a nuclear attack. At the same time, the Indian government has come up with innovative statements and actions that signal that it does have military-diplomatic options to counter Pakistan's moves. In terms of statements, India unveiled the military plan "Cold Start", designed to respond to Pakistani aggression with quick mobilization of select military units (Ladwig 2007–2008). There have been hints that India's NFU declaration has been modified to allow for nuclear first use under some circumstances (Shukla 2017). India has also undertaken actions that signal its will to react. For instance, in 2016, India carried out a semi-covert operation using Special Forces across the Line of Control with Pakistan, dubbed a "surgical strike". This small-scale operation was in response to an attack on Indian military personnel a few days earlier.

Reassurance in Four Crises

Threats are avidly discussed during and after crises, but reassurance, being more subtle, receives less attention. The following section discusses four crises in the period of formal nuclear weapon possession.

1999: The Kargil War

The 1998 tests were followed by a period where Pakistan and India entered into discussions ("the Lahore talks") that were meant to show that they could manage nuclear tensions in a responsible way. These talks were still underway when incursions were detected in the Kargil sector of the border in May 1999. Military personnel from the Pakistan Army (Northern Light Infantry) and insurgents had occupied the mountain heights. The government of Pakistan denied its involvement for several weeks (Kumar 1999). Indian armed forces mobilized to regain control of the heights. Three months of intense conventional fighting followed, sparking fears that a nuclear weapon would actually be used for the first time after 1945 (Dugger 2002). During the crisis, both parties issued veiled nuclear threats. Pakistan hinted that it was on the brink of using nuclear weapons.

The goal was probably to heighten the probability of US/international intervention and end hostilities quickly – in a longer war; Indian strength in conventional weapons is likely to prevail. On the Indian side, the Chief of Naval Staff declared that India was fully prepared to counter nuclear strikes (Anon 1999). India moved some missiles, and also increased the alert status of its forces (Narang 2014, 270–71; Ramana 2003). At the same time, India sent signals of reassurance to Pakistan, and to the international audience. Indian leaders were convinced of the importance of staying behind Pakistan's "red lines" or threshold for nuclear use. They were also mindful of the international audience: their behavior in the Kargil conflict was the first test of the 1998 Indian assertions that nuclear weapons would be used only as a last resort. India signaled the limited nature of its response in several ways.

First, it kept its forces on the Indian side of the LoC, and limited its conventional operations. Second, civilian authorities stipulated that the air force refrain from attacking assets on the Pakistani side of the LoC, even though this probably heightened Indian casualties (Roychowdhury and Singh 1999). Over five hundred Indian soldiers lost their lives in the Kargil conflict (Pande 2005, 27). In the aftermath, some military leaders and analysts criticized the government for this choice. They claimed that lives had been needlessly lost because of the restrictions on airpower (Datta 2005). As Manoj Joshi puts it, Pakistani nuclear weapons compelled India to restrict itself to the narrow killing field that Pakistan had created (Joshi 1999). Third, Indian combat activities were restricted to the Kargil sector; a second front was not opened up (Bell and Macdonald 2019). When queried by the military about the possibility of attacking Pakistan elsewhere, Indian Prime

Minister Vajpayee reportedly responded with a simple statement to the effect that the other side had a bomb (Narang 2014, 272). It is important to note that public opinion in India supported crossing the Line of Control in 'hot pursuit" of the infiltrators and attacking terrorist camps on the other side. The Bharatiya Janata Party (BJP) government eschewed these options.

Also, to be noted: Kargil was South Asia's first "media war", with the Indian press and television channels showing a distinct bellicose bias (Manchanda 2001). The conflict was playing out shortly before the relatively weak interim government headed into national elections. We can see that reassurance took priority over the imperatives of domestic politics. India also signaled to the international community that, in contrast to Pakistan, its behavior was rational and responsible. India's ambassador to Washington called Pakistan the "epicenter of international terrorism". He held it responsible for terrorist training camps, the growth of "terrorist factories", and "nuclear blackmail". He contrasted this with India's choices, such as adherence to the NFU policy (Sardesai 2003). India's National Security Adviser highlighted the role of democratic institutions, declaring that Kargil had "demonstrated that our system and the political leadership believe in great responsibility and restraint, as you would expect from the largest democracy in the world" (Sidhu 2007, 145).

The Indian handling of the crisis was praised by the United States (Singh 2007). Whereas India's stances during crises marked it as a mature country, Western fears of nuclear escalation boomeranged on Pakistan (Guha 1999; Karnad 2002, 145). Eventually, Pakistan's miscalculations regarding the international reaction to its armed incursion turned the tactical victory scored at Kargil into a strategic defeat. The intervention of US President Bill Clinton in July 1999 forced Pakistan's civilian Prime Minister to order a withdrawal from Kargil (Riedel 2002).

The 2001–02 Border Standoff

A small convoy of vehicles unsuccessfully attempted to storm the Indian Parliament in December 2001. The Indian government accused the group Jaish-e-Mohammed of carrying out the daring attack, and demanded the extradition of several operatives allegedly residing in Pakistan. The demand was backed up with the largest Indian troop mobilization since the 1971 war, codenamed Operation Parakram. Approximately 800,000 Indian troops were mobilized on the border for several months, facing off with Pakistani soldiers (Narang 2009). Indian public opinion was inflamed by the attack on Parliament, and further by a May 2002 assault on the Kaluchak camp, which housed the families of military personnel.

Again, there were strident demands that the government pursue military action against Pakistan. According to retired Pakistani military intelligence chief, General Durrani, the Vajpayee government in New Delhi faced a "minimum political necessity" to mobilize Indian troops (Dulat, Durrani, and Sinha 2018, 215). Prime Minister Vajpayee's party was facing four crucial state elections at the time. In a televised address, Vajpayee issued signals of threat, declaring that this time the battle against terrorism would be fought in a decisive manner (Anon 2001). Both India and Pakistan stated that all options were being considered (Gardiner 2002). As a result of this and other threats, nuclear war seemed a distinct possibility. Some scholars drew the lesson that India had become more comfortable with issuing nuclear threats. V.R. Raghavan has described the 2002 mobilization as proof that Indian strategy, influenced by the response to 9/11 by the United States, "had graduated from defensive to proactive, offensive responses to terrorism" (Raghavan 2004).

Although the 2001–02 crises featured several threatening signals, there were some signals of reassurance as well. First, as in 1999, India signaled that the deployment was rational, and specifically a response to the Parliament attack. Even when Pakistani President Musharraf declared to a German magazine that he would use an atomic weapon if Pakistan's existence were threatened, India did not respond (Roy Choudhury 2004). Second, India continued adherence to routine confidence building measures: less than three weeks after the attack, on the first day of 2002, New Delhi exchanged with Islamabad navigational coordinates of their nuclear installations and facilities, as they had done for the past thirteen years in accordance with the 1998 Agreement on the Prohibition of Attack against Nuclear Installations and Facilities. India also notified Pakistan in advance about a test of its Medium Range Ballistic Missile, Agni, as per the 1999 Lahore Memorandum of Understanding (Roy Choudhury 2004). Third, Indian troops did not cross the border or the Line of Control, aside from an action to repulse an alleged probe by Pakistan army personnel, intruding 800 metres inside the Neelam sector in Kashmir (Mehta 2003).

Finally, the government realized that partisan politics or parochial organizational concerns should not be allowed to influence signaling. In January 2002, the Chief of Army Staff, General Padmanabhan, made a statement about retaliation against a nuclear strike. Within hours, in an unprecedented public counter to the military, India's Defence Minister cautioned against handling nuclear issues "in a cavalier manner" and sought to dispel "uncalledfor concerns" about the General's statement (Roy Choudhury 2004). At times, India's signaling became complicated. On May 22, the Indian Prime Minister, declared to troops: "the time has come for a decisive battle and we will have a sure victory in this battle".

It is probable that Vajpayee intended to boost the morale of personnel, who had been at the highest level of operational readiness for five months. However, the statement was perceived as threatening, both in Islamabad and in Washington (Roy Choudhury 2004). In the international community, India garnered sympathy as a victim of terrorism, particularly as a democracy fighting terrorism. Indian leaders cited the precedent of the United States invading Iraq with the goal of pre-empting terrorist attacks (Anon 2002). Foreign Minister Yashwant Sinha drew a clear parallel, stating: "If lack of democracy, possessing weapons of mass destruction and export of terrorism are criterion, Pakistan is a fit case for pre-emptive strike" (Anon 2003). Gaurav Kampani writes that "India was able to frame the insurgency in Kashmir as a war between a multicultural democracy and monocultural sectarianism" (Kampani 2002).

2008: The Mumbai Attacks

On 26 November 2008, a small group of militants belonging to the militant Islamist group Lashkar-e-Taiba – which had been banned by the Pakistani government during the 2002 border standoff – launched a daring sea assault from Karachi, Pakistan. The target was again Mumbai. A series of simultaneous attacks targeted hospitals, railway stations, areas frequented by foreign tourists, and Jewish sites. Over 160 lives were lost. The world feared that the Manmohan Singh government in New Delhi – a few months away from a tough general election – would retaliate with military action, that could escalate to nuclear war. During this tense period, Pakistani officials at one point seriously feared a surprise air attack, and at another were shaken by a hoax caller pretending to be the Indian Foreign Minister (Abbas 2008; Coll 2009).

In India, some former bureaucrats and military personnel, as well as media pundits, called for conducting "limited military strikes" across the Line of Control, perhaps using special forces or so-called smart bombs (Raghavan and Chaudhuri 2008). In the event, India's response was extraordinarily restrained. New Delhi did not mobilize military forces to retaliate against Lashkar camps operating in Pakistan. The civilian authorities in New Delhi rejected a proposal by the Air Force to bomb these camps (Singh and Chaudhuri 2011). Pakistan was presumably reassured when India did not mobilize troops. However, India put diplomatic pressure on Pakistan both directly, and through the United States, China, and Saudi Arabia (Nayak and Krepon 2012, 46). The government, headed by the Congress Prime Minister Manmohan Singh, faced accusations that it was bowing to US pressure and going easy on Pakistan.

However, according to Vipin Narang, there is little to suggest that pressure from Washington stopped India's leaders. The US put pressure on Pakistan – not India – to rein in militant groups. Narang posits that nuclear deterrence worked: that Pakistan's asymmetric escalation posture inhibited Indian leaders from executing militarily effective retaliatory options that might have otherwise been considered (Narang 2010, 121). A former Indian

Chief of Army Staff, General Shankar Roychowdhury, bluntly stated that Pakistan's threat of early nuclear first-use deterred India from seriously considering conventional military strikes (Narang 2010, 84). The few accounts that exist of decision-making in New Delhi in November and December 2008, confirm that the specter of nuclear retaliation stayed the hand of revenge (Rabasa et al. 2009).

According to interviews conducted by Pranab Samanta, "the unpredictability on the Pakistan side and the fear that its decision makers could opt for a disproportionate response, including the nuclear option, stymied any possible chance of military action" (Samanta 2010). Signals of reassurance also sought to convince major foreign powers that India was not about to take precipitate military action. These signals opened up the space for world leaders – who had an interest in condemning support of terrorism and nuclear use – to focus on Pakistan instead. That is, the military option became less attractive partly because there was adequate pressure on Pakistan from the international community – particularly after the interception of messages between the attackers on the ground and their controllers in Pakistan – to open an investigation. Indian leaders concluded that "military force ought to be used only as the last resort, and efforts mounted first to exert international pressure to make support for terror very costly for Pakistan" (Thapar 2008).

2016: "Surgical" Strikes In an early morning attack on 18 September 2016, armed militants targeted an army camp in Uri, a garrison town close to the LoC and killed 19 Indian soldiers. The Indian government claimed that items bearing Pakistani markings were found at the site, and held the organization Jaish-e-Mohammad responsible for the attack (Peri 2016). Later, another organization, Lashkar-e-Taiba, was identified as carrying out the attack (Tiwary 2017). Considering that the BJP was again in power, this time under Prime Minister Narendra Modi – a known hardliner on the issue of Pakistan – there were fears of escalation. Moreover, Modi's party, the BJP, was facing elections in several states within a few months.

Ten days after the Uri attacks, India struck back with simultaneous raids targeting training camps for terrorists in Pakistan Occupied Kashmir. This meant that troops crossed the LoC. It is estimated that 70–80 men (both uniformed personnel and others not in uniform) were killed in these raids (Gokhale 2017, loc. 735). It must be noted that there is considerable doubt and confusion about the location of the targets and number of casualties in the raids (Kapur 2018, 73). On 29 September 2016, the Director-General of Military Operations (DGMO) of the Indian Army made a statement to the media, at a rare joint press conference of the Ministries of Defence and External Affairs (Anon 2016a). This statement contains several signals of reassurance, although it concludes with a clear signal of threat for the future:

. . . the Indian Armed Forces are fully prepared for any contingency that may arise. It is India's intention to maintain peace and tranquillity in the region. But we cannot allow the terrorists to operate across the Line of Control with impunity and attack citizens of our country at will. . . we expect the Pakistani army to cooperate with us to erase the menace of terrorism from the region.

The statement reads:

Based on very credible and specific information which we received yesterday that some terrorist teams had positioned themselves at launch pads along the Line of Control with an aim to carry out infiltration and terrorist strikes in Jammu & Kashmir and in various other metros in our country, the Indian army conducted surgical strikes last night at these launch pads. The operations were basically focused to ensure that these terrorists do not succeed in their design of infiltration and carrying out destruction and endangering the lives of citizens of our country.

We note that the DGMO's statement claims that the operation was carried out on the basis of information about specific terrorist plots. He refers to "launchpads", a more technical sounding term than "militant training facilities" or "terrorist camps". He uses terms such as "specific", "credible", "focused", and "positioned" to heighten this impression. All of these terms contribute to the understanding of this military operation as "surgical". Moreover, the statement is carefully crafted to portray a rational response and remove any impression that India was lashing out in anger:

The matter had been taken up at highest diplomatic levels and through military channels. India has also offered consular access to these apprehended terrorists for Pakistan to verify their confessions. Furthermore, we had proposed that fingerprints and DNA samples of terrorists killed in Punch and Uri could be made available to Pakistan for investigation. Despite our persistent urging that Pakistan respect its January 2004 commitment for not allowing its soil or territory under its control to be used for terrorism against India, there has been no let up.

Finally, the statement emphasizes limited scope: "The operations aimed at neutralizing terrorists have since ceased. We do not have any plans for further continuation". A former head of the Pakistani military intelligence service, General Durrani, described the strikes as a face-saving device for the government in New Delhi, which was confronting an uncontrollable upsurge in militancy in Kashmir. Durrani went on to suggest that although the Indian military action was closer to hot pursuit than a "surgical strike", being cognizant of the constraints on the India government, Pakistan wisely accepted the description (Dulat, Durrani, and Sinha 2018, 210). In what appears to be a case of what Austin Carson calls "tacit collusion", Pakistan refrained from publicizing the covert activity by India as a way of resisting pressure from its own citizens to escalate (Carson 2016). Interestingly, while opposition parties in India demanded proof of the raid, the government did not release video footage of the raid until June 2018. Upon this release, government ministers proclaimed that the delay showed that there had been no intention of garnering political mileage during the election campaign (Anon 2018). It is also possible that the footage was not released during the crisis period to avoid exacerbating calls for revenge in Pakistan.

Balancing Threat and Reassurance: Sustainable in South Asia?

Nuclear optimists would view the description of reassurance presented above as proof that deterrence works. However, such a conclusion would be unwarranted. First, the analysis in this paper has only dealt with nuclear reassurance signaling from India. Pakistan may have very different motivations during crises. It may be rational for Pakistan to signal that is highly motivated to use nuclear weapons – regardless of whether it truly intends to – to trigger intervention by outside powers like the United States. Pakistan may also choose not to "receive" Indian signals of reassurance, depending on its civil-military dynamics and electoral cycle. Second, even in cases where India and Pakistan are seeking to avoid war, reassurance may be inadequate to prevent war for the three reasons listed here. The section concludes with a consideration of steps to bolster reassurance.

Complexity: Multiple Audiences

Unlike in the Cold War strategic situation where the United States and the Soviet Union were in dialogue primarily with each other, the deterrence game in South Asia has both sub-state (such as militant groups) and extra-regional players (like China and the United States). Consequently, the signals that Indian and Pakistani leaders wish to convey are received by multiple audiences. One could imagine a scenario in which an Indian statement succeeds in reassuring Pakistan, but emboldens China; or another where the Pakistani military pulls back in the face of a credible threat, but the same massive threat pushes insurgents over the edge and triggers a surge in suicide attacks. Especially problematic are sub-state actors (say, those targeted by a surgical strike), since they are not necessarily under the control of state actors. Stephen Tankel, writing about the Lashkar-e-Taiba, has pointed out that since Pakistan's proxies operate without critical oversight from their handlers in order to maintain plausible deniability, they could inadvertently cross India's red lines (Tankel 2011, 113).

This discussion points to the need for a clear channel of trusted communication. During the 2001–02 border standoffs, both countries withdrew their High Commissioners (Ambassadors) and halved the strength of their diplomatic missions (Roy Choudhury 2004). This weakened formal diplomatic channels. Retired intelligence chiefs Dulat and Durrani have suggested that Indian and Pakistani intelligence services set up a mechanism for coordination, which in the event of an incident such as the Mumbai attacks, would exchange information that could avert a nuclear exchange (Dulat and Durrani 2011). They even suggest that, given advance warning and discussion, Pakistan would accept a "choreographed response", which could include bombing of three or four places on its territory, as an Indian response to a Mumbai-style attack (Dulat, Durrani, and Sinha 2018, 212). A second policy implication is for the international audience, which wants to see signals of reassurance.

In the midst of a crisis, intensive diplomacy by the United States or the European Union may in fact throw off the delicate balance between threat and reassurance. Having a solid diplomatic presence in both countries, and building strong relationships with civilian and military authorities prior to any crisis, would be the optimal practice for international actors. This is particularly important in the case of Pakistan, which has endured diplomatic disengagement from the United States over disagreements over counter-terrorism operations.

Imprecision: Doctrine and Force Development

India's goal is to conceive of military operations that stay under Pakistan's red lines. However, neither are these lines clearly drawn, nor is it in Pakistan's interest to clarify them. In 2002, a top decision-maker in Pakistan, General Khalid Kidwai, conveyed the message that even political destabilization or economic strangulation of Pakistan would be cause for nuclear use (Pugwash Conferences on Science and World Affairs 2002). By keeping the nuclear threshold low and uncertain, Pakistan can deter a wider range of enemy actions. Therefore, signals of reassurance, however carefully crafted, are drawing on misleading information. Take the example of the Line of Control (LoC), the de facto border. A former Pakistani President, Pervez Musharraf, is on record that even a step across the LoC by India would trigger a nuclear war. Mark Bell and Julia Macdonald see this example of clear communication of red lines. In their case study of Kargil, this clarity, among other factors, leads them to classify that 1999 conflict as a "staircase crisis" with controlled escalation (Bell and Macdonald 2019, 19). However, in September 2016, India's so-called surgical strikes did cross the LoC (and in fact may have attacked targets at quite some distance inside Pakistan-held territory).

It appears that the LoC is no longer a true firebreak on the ladder of nuclear escalation. A lack of clarity is also noted in the matter of India's NFU pledge. This was a key element of its reassurance strategy, right from the start of India's existence as a declared nuclear power. However, it appears that in an attempt to signal that it retains multiple options to respond militarily to Pakistani moves, India has modified the NFU. In 2003, the Draft Nuclear Doctrine (which incidentally was never formalized) suggested that India reserved the right to respond to biological or chemical attacks with nuclear weapons. In 2016, India's Cabinet Minister for Defence, Manohar Parrikar expressed his personal opposition to the NFU policy. Today, the parameters of the Indian NFU are unclear (Narang and Clary 2016). This leads to confusion, which may lead Pakistani decision-makers, expecting an Indian first strike in a crisis, to strike first. The analysis in the paper has focused on both actions and statements that signal reassurance.

While India's statements continue to be reassuring, certain actions in the domain of military development appear threatening to Pakistan – especially because they are neither discussed openly nor integrated with a broader strategy. Vipin Narang points to the incongruence between the declared strategy of assured retaliation, and India's plans to develop ballistic missile defense systems and multiple independently targetable warheads. Although these plans are in their infancy, and are potentially countering Chinese rather than Pakistani moves, decision-makers in Islamabad are forced to consider the Indian plans as part of a counterforce strategy against their assets (Narang 2018). The imprecision inherent in the formulation used "minimum deterrent" or "credible minimum deterrent" fosters the potential hijacking of policy by organizational interests in the military or defense scientific establishment.

Political Pressure: Reaction to Attacks

Three of the four crises described above (in December 2001, November 2008, and September 2016) were triggered by attacks on Indian soil by terrorists allegedly backed by Pakistan. The Kargil conflict had a much stronger link to the Pakistani government. In all four cases, the government in New Delhi faced intense pressure from its citizens for a dramatic military strike against Pakistan. It is to be noted that the pressure has been on an upward trend: in 2016 a surprisingly large percentage of poll respondents were even willing to face nuclear annihilation to punish Pakistan for the Uri attacks (Anon 2016c). Political pressure stems from three main sources. First, Indians are dismayed over the inability of the government to secure the borders and prevent attacks on innocent civilians.

For instance, a mere two months after the post-Parliament attack border standoff in 2001–02, Defence Minister George Fernandes was forced to admit in Parliament that many of the terrorist camps in Pakistan, which were closed or relocated to interior areas during July–August 2002, had re-opened (Pande 2005, 30). Second, politicians exploit the feeling of frustration among citizens by making untenable promises to end cross-border activity and terrorism. For instance, a top leader, Amit Shah, promised during the 2014 national election campaign that there would be no such intrusions under a BJP government (Anon 2014). Each regime in New Delhi faces greater pressure to threaten Pakistan than its predecessor did. A few months after the so-called surgical strikes, two Indian Army personnel were killed (and their bodies apparently mutilated) on the LoC (Das and Roche 2017). The Modi government once again came under pressure to punish Pakistan and/or its proxies, but managed to stave off the pressure (Talukdar 2017).

Third, as retired intelligence chiefs Dulat and Durrani point out, the media (in particular television and social media) profit by inflaming public sentiment and heightening the danger of war (Dulat, Durrani, and Sinha 2018, 213). Reflecting on the publicity around the 2016 strikes, a retired senior military officer noted that even successful operations can become a burden, as they raise expectations when the next crisis occurs (Chinna 2018). From this, we can conclude that signals of reassurance are likely to be perceived by domestic audiences as signs of political weakness. In a future nuclear crisis, Indian authorities may not be motivated to transmit reassuring signals, and this will endanger the delicate balance of threat and reassurance.

Bolstering Reassurance

In the long term, only a comprehensive dialogue between India and Pakistan, which takes up the core dispute over Kashmir, but also addresses other burning issues such as sponsorship of terrorism, support of sub-national insurgency, water rights disputes, bilateral arms control and verification, etc., would lead to a lasting peace. However, we may consider bolstering the signaling of reassurance in nuclear crises for the short to medium term. Sub-national and extra-national actors are part of the audience for signaling. The national leadership in both countries should be aware of the dangers inherent in using non-state actors against adversaries– what has been called the "riding the tiger" phenomenon. During crises, these non-state actors must be included in the loop and governments should attempt to keep a tight rein on their activities. The United States and other major powers should be aware of the existence of multiple audiences, and adjust their expectations accordingly. For example, pressing leaders to apologize or deescalate may have unexpected, negative consequences.

Imprecision has been identified as a major issue in signaling reassurance. Imprecision can be remedied in non-crisis periods, by expanding Confidence Building Measures to include discussions of terminology used for routine troop movements, terms used by military and politicians, and even trusted media outlets. The last obstacle that was identified – political pressure on governments to issue threats rather than reassurance–is the hardest to tackle. The publics of both countries should be educated on the costs and consequences of nuclear war in South Asia. The media have a vital role in this regard, in addition to refraining from inflammatory statements and speculation during crises. A model code of conduct could be drawn up by a bilateral committee and responsible media outlets could sign on to it. Most importantly, politicians must eschew ultranationalist posturing, both during crises and otherwise.

Conclusion

In March 2000, in the aftermath of the Kargil conflict, then-US President Bill Clinton described South Asia as the most dangerous place on earth. The Indian President responded by terming such descriptions alarmist and counter-productive (Marcus 2000). By analyzing four crises between India and Pakistan, the paper has highlighted that India's behavior in crises includes both threat and reassurance. Although scholars and policy-makers are less likely to discuss signals of reassurance than threats, reassurance has played a role in ensuring that the India-Pakistan crises do not "go nuclear" in the sense of a nuclear exchange. At the same time, the paper also discussed three factors that impede signals of reassurance, and cautioned that the balance between threat and reassurance is too delicate to be relied on to keep the peace between India and Pakistan.

Disclosure Statement

No potential conflict of interest was reported by the author.

Notes on Contributor

Karthika Sasikumar is Associate Professor of Political Science at San Jose State University. Originally from India, Dr. Sasikumar received her Ph.D. from the Government Department at Cornell University in 2006. Her dissertation explores the interaction between India and the international nuclear nonproliferation order. Her current research and teaching interests are in International Relations theory, international regimes, global security, migration, and national identity. India-Pakistan Crises under the Nuclear Shadow: The Role of Reassurance Karthika Sasikumar To cite this article: Karthika Sasikumar (2019) India-Pakistan Crises under the Nuclear Shadow: The Role of Reassurance, Journal for Peace and Nuclear Disarmament,2:1,151-169,DOI:10.1080/25751654.2019.1619229. To-link-to-this-article: https://doi.org/10.1080/25751654.2019.16 19229 © 2019 The Author(s). Published by Informa UK Limited, trading as Taylor & Francis Group on behalf of the Nagasaki University. Accepted author version posted online: 22 May 2019. Published online: 04 Jun 2019. JOURNAL FOR PEACE AND NUCLEAR DISARMAMENT 2019, VOL. 2, NO. 1, 151–169 https://doi.org/10.1080/25751654.2019.1619229. CONTACT: Karthika Sasikumar karthika.sasikumar@sjsu.edu Department of Political Science, San José State University, One Washington Square, San José, CA 95192, USA JOURNAL FOR PEACE AND NUCLEAR DISARMAMENT 2019, VOL. 2, NO. 1, 151–169 https://doi.org/10 .1080/25751654.2019.1619229 © 2019 The Author(s). Published by Informa UK Limited, trading as Taylor & Francis Group on behalf of the Nagasaki University. This is an Open Access article distributed under the terms of the Creative Commons Attribution License (http:// creativecommons.org/licenses/ by/4.0/), which permits unrestricted use, distribution, and reproduction in any medium, provided the original work is properly cited.

Notes to Chapters

Chapter 1: Modern Nuclear Technology and the Danger of Nuclear War in South Asia

1.   Thomas G. Mahnken Travis Sharp Grace B.KIM (2020)

2.   17 August 2014, Mr. Assange made public an email in which Hillary Clinton urged the then advisor to US President Barak Obama, Mr. John Podesta, to pressure Qatar and Saudi Arabia for funding Islamic State (ISIS).

3.   Maxim Suchkov, Sim Tack (The Future of War, Valdai Discussion Club Report, August 2019)

4.   Ben Aris. 08 May 2019

5.   29 April 2020; VOA

6.   Federation of American Scientists warned January 2020

7.   Ibid

8.   Scott Ritter, RT News, 28 April, 2020

9.   Asia Times, Rechard Javad Heydarian 25 May 2020

10.   Musa Khan Jalalzai, March 2015, Daily Times

11.   18 May 2020, TASS News

12.   Ibid

Chapter-2: Pakistan's Nuclear Weapons and South Asia

1.   Pakistan: Living with a Nuclear Monkey. Musa Khan Jalalzaai, 2018

2.   Mahmudul Huque 1 February 2020

3.   Pakistan: Living with a Nuclear Monkey. Musa Khan Jalalzaai, 2018

4.   Mahmudul Huque 1 February 2020

5.   Due to continual mistrust between the two countries, each would be likely to misinterpret military movements, missiles tests, or acciden-

tal detonations as an impending attack by the other side. Nathan E Busch

6. The Guardian 26 September 2019

7. Ibid

8. Siddharthya Roy, The Diplomat, 05 November, 2019

9. Khuldune Shahid, Diplomat, June 18, 2019

10. April 18, 2015, IS claimed to have carried out a deadly suicide attack in Jalalabad in which 40 people were and 125 injured

11. Ibid

12. Ibid

13. Reuters 18 November 2014

14. Dawn 11 December 2014

15. December 13, 2014, in an interview with a local television channel, the chief of the Red Mosque, Maulana Abdul Aziz, confirmed the video message of his seminary students.

Chapter-3: Nuclearization and Military Confrontation between India, Pakistan and China

1. Richard Purcell 28 January 2020-Global Security Review

2. Analyst Marianne Schneider-Petsinger highlighted aspects of trade war and technological competition between China and the United States

3. Ravi Agrawal paper

4. June 6, 2015, Pajhwok News

5. Mir Sajad Modern diplomacy 29 May 2020

6. Haris Bilal Malik, Modern Diplomacy 28 May 2020

7. George PerKovich and Toby Dalton, 2015

8. Bilal Malik Modern Diplomacy 28 May 2020

Chapter 4: Prospects for Cooperation on Tackling Nuclear and Radiological Terrorism in South Asia: India–Pakistan Nuclear Detection Architecture. Muhammad Umer Khan

1. B. Subrat, Terrorism in India: Domestic and External Influence. India Int. J. Interdiscip.Multidiscip. Stud. (2014), (available athttp://

www.ijims.com/uploads/696780174f19c7634e08zppd_2014411.
pdf).

2. Dawn.com, Pakistan says evidence of Balochistan interference
shared with India (2013), (availableat http://www.dawn.com/
news/1047628)

3. Nuclear & Radiological Terrorism. Fed. Am. Sci. (2016), (available at
https://fas.org/issues/nuclearand-radiological-terrorism/).

4. Z. Laub, Pakistan's New Generation of Terrorists. Counc. Foreign
Relat. (2013), (available athttp://www.cfr.org/pakistan/pakistans-
new-generation-terrorists/p15422).

5. A. Pashupati, Al Qaeda Launches Wing in Indian Subcontinent.
NDTV.com (2014), (available at http://www.ndtv.com/india-news/
al-qaeda-launches-wing-in-indian-subcontinent-658803).

6. F. the Newspaper, Attack on GHQ: confessions of a terrorist mas-
termind. Dawn.com (2011), (available at http://www.dawn.
com/2011/09/21/attack-on-ghq-confessions-of-a-terroristmaster-
mind/).

7. Y. Lukov, A. Lawson, As it happened: Pakistan school attack. BBC
News (2014), (available at http://www.bbc.com/news/live/world-
asia-30491113).

8. H. Manan, Taliban threat: Nuclear site in DG Khan cordoned off. Express Trib. (2012), (available at http://tribune.com.pk/story/432295/
taliban-threat-nuclear-site-in-dg-khan-cordoned-off/).

9. H. Haqqani, The Ideologies of South Asian Jihadi Groups. Carn-
egieendowment.org (2016), (available at http://carnegieendowment.
org/files/Ideologies.pdf).

10. D. Rassler, Al-Qa`ida's Pakistan Strategy. Combat. Terror.
Cent. (2009), (available at https://www.ctc.usma.edu/posts/al-
qaida%e2%80%99s-pakistan-strategy).

11. Karachi, Escalation: Links between violent sectarian groups and the
Pakistani Taliban are growing. The Economist (2012), (available at
http://www.economist.com/news/21567422-links-betweenviolent-
sectarian-groups-and-pakistani-taliban-are-growing-escalation).

12. R. Barrett, The al-Qaeda-Taliban Nexus. Counc. Foreign Relat.
(2009), (available at http://www.cfr.org/pakistan/al-qaeda-taliban-
nexus/p20838).

13. B. Raman, How Significant is Khalid Sheikh's arrest? Rediff. com (2003), (available at http://www.rediff.com/news/2003/mar/03raman.htm).

14. I. Tharoor, Why al-Qaeda is opening a new wing in South Asia. Wash. Post (2014), (available at https://www.washingtonpost.com/blogs/worldviews/wp/2014/09/03/why-al-qaeda-is-opening-anew-wing-in-south-asia).

15. AQIS Clarifies Targets of Karachi Naval Yard Attack as U.S., Indian Navies. Site Intell. Group (2014), (available at https://news.siteintelgroup.com/Jihadist-News/aqis-clarifies-targets-of-karachinaval-yard-attack-as-u-s-indian-navies.html).

16. IAEA Incident and Trafficking Database (ITDB): Incidents of nuclear and other radioactive material out of regulatory control (2016), (available at http://wwwns.iaea.org/downloads/security/itdb-fact-sheet.pdf).

17. Incident and Trafficking Database (ITDB), (available at http://www-ns.iaea.org/security/itdb.asp).

18. IAEA, Nuclear Safety and Security, (available at http://www-ns.iaea.org/security/itdb.asp).

19. C. D. Ferguson, Nuclear energy: what everyone needs to know (Oxford University Press, Oxford ;New York, 2011), What everyone needs to know.

20. MacArthur Foundation, Harvard's Matthew Bunn on Nuclear Terrorism: Enhancing Nuclear Security | MacArthur Foundation (2012; https://www.youtube.com/watch?v=6QBarfleQ-A).

21. H. Khan, K. P. S. Menon, Agreement between India and Pakistan on the prohibition of attack against nuclear installations and facilities (India-Pakistan non-attack agreement) (2016), (availableat http://www.nti.org/media/pdfs/aptindpak.pdf).

22. Lahore Declaration (2016), (available at http://www.nti.org/media/pdfs/aptlahore.pdf).

23. S. Padder, The Composite Dialogue between India and Pakistan: Structure, Process and Agency.Heidelb. Pap. South Asian Comp. Polit. 65 (2012) (available at http://archiv.ub.uniheidelberg.de/volltextserver/13143/).

24. M. Kugelman, R. Hathaway, Pakistan-India Trade: What Needs to Be Done? What Does It Matter? Wilson Cent. (2013), (available at

https://www.wilsoncenter.org/publication/pakistan-india-trade-what-needs-to-be-done-what-does-it-matter).

25. S. Sengupta, India and Pakistan Open Kashmir Trade Route. N. Y. Times (2008), (available athttp://www.nytimes.com/2008/10/22/world/asia/22kashmir.html).

26. India-Pakistan border post opens for business. Al Jazeera (2012), (available athttp://www.aljazeera.com/news/asia/2012/04/201241343825570512.html).

27. Countering Nuclear Terrorism: How DNDO Supports Detection and Forensics | Tactical Defense Media. Tactical Def. Media (2016), (available at http://tacticaldefensemedia.com/counteringnuclear-terrorism-how-dndo-supports-detection-and-forensics/).

28. IAEA Nuclear Security Series No. 2: Nuclear Forensics Support. IAEA.org (2006), (available at http://www-pub.iaea.org/MTCD/Publications/PDF/Pub1241_web.pdf).

29. Global Initiative to Combat Nuclear Terrorism Fact Sheet. GICNT (2016), (available at http://www.state.gov/documents/organization/145499.pdf).

30. Global Initiative to Combat Nuclear Terrorism (GICNT). NTI.org (2015), (available at http://www.nti.org/learn/treaties-and-regimes/global-initiative-combat-nuclear-terrorism-gicnt/).

31. IAEA Nuclear Security Series No. 15: Nuclear Security Recommendations on Nuclear and Other Radioactive Material out of Regulatory Control. IAEA.org (2011), (available at http://wwwpub.iaea.org/MTCD/publications/PDF/Pub1488_web.pdf).

32. D. Smith, Development of a National Nuclear Forensics Library (2015).

33. Nuclear Forensics: Role, State of the Art, Program Needs (2016), (available at http://www.aps.org/policy/reports/popa-reports/upload/nuclear-forensics.pdf).

34. J. Goldberg, M. Ambinder, The Pentagon's Secret Plans to Secure Pakistan's Nuclear Arsenal (2011), (available at http://www.nti.org/gsn/article/the-pentagons-secret-plans-to-secure-pakistansnuclear-arsenal/).

35. A. Gul, As Pakistan Expands Nuclear Program, China Seen as Most Reliable Partner. VOA (2014), (available at http://www.voanews.

com/a/as-pakistan-expands-nuclear-program-china-seen-as-mostreliable-partner/1912529.html).

36. Z. Jiegen, China-Pakistan Nuclear Relation after the Cold War and Its International Implications.Program Strateg. Stab. Eval. (2016), (available at http://www.posse.gatech.edu/sites/default/files/pub-files/ChinaPakistan%20Nuclear%20Relation%20after%20the%20 Cold%20War%20and%20Its%20Internation al%20Implications. pdf).

37. T. V. Paul, Chinese-Pakistani Nuclear/Missile Ties and the Balance of Power. Nonproliferation Rev.(2003), (available at http://www. nonproliferation.org/wp-content/uploads/npr/102paul.pdf).

38. J. Bajoria, E. Pan, The U.S.-India Nuclear Deal. Counc. Foreign Relat. (2010), (available at http://www.cfr.org/india/us-india-nuclear-deal/ p9663).

39. S. Amer Latif, U.S.-India Counterterrorism Cooperation: Deepening the Partnership: Statement before the House Foreign Affairs Committee, Subcommittee on Terrorism, Nonproliferation, and Trade. Cent. Strateg. Int. Stud. (2011), (available at https://csis-prod. s3.amazonaws.com/s3fspublic/legacy_files/files/ts110914_Latif. pdf).

40. U.S.-India Joint Statement – "Shared Effort; Progress for All." whitehouse.gov (2015), (available at https://www.whitehouse.gov/ the-pressoffice/2015/01/25/us-india-joint-statement-shared-effort-progress-all).

41. A. Aneja, India, U.S. discuss n-safety issues. The Hindu (2016), (available at http://www.thehindu.com/2002/03/30/sto-ries/2002033002061100.htm).

42. Mobile Radiological Laboratory. Dep. At. Energy (2016), (available at http://dae.nic.in/?q=node/303).

43. Electronics Corporation of India Limited: Radiation Detectors and Instrumentation Division. Electron. Corp. India Ltd. (2016), (available at http://www.ecil.co.in/RID_Images/RID_Prouct_Profile.pdf).

44. J. Shenoy, Portal radiation monitors to give India a radiation shield at exit points - Times of India. Times India (2014), (available at http://timesofindia.indiatimes.com/city/mangaluru/Portalradia-tion-monitors-to-give-India-a-radiation-shield-at-exit-points/ar-ticleshow/38622584.cms).

45. S. Mishra, M. Ahmed, Cooperative Measures to Support the Indo-Pak Agreement on Reducing Risk from Accidents Relating to Nuclear Weapons. Sandia.gov (2014), (available at http://www.sandia.gov/cooperative-monitoring-center/_assets/documents/sand2014-2607.pdf).

46. Pakistan Nuclear Regulatory Authority, School for Nuclear and Radiation Safety, (available at http://www.pnra.org/snrs/SNRS%20Brochure.pdf).

47. United Nations Security Council Resolution 1540 (2016), (available at http://www.un.org/en/sc/1540/).

48. NTI, U.S.: President Signs Nuclear Forensics and Attribution Act. NTI.org (2012), (available athttp://www.nti.org/analysis/articles/us-president-signs-nuclear-forensics-and-attribution-act/).

49. H.R. 730 (111th): Nuclear Forensics and Attribution Act. GovTrack.us (2010), (available at https://www.govtrack.us/congress/bills/111/hr730/text).

50. D. P. Fidler, S. Ganguly, India Wants to Join the Non-Proliferation Treaty as a Weapon State. YaleGlobal Online (2010), (available at http://yaleglobal.yale.edu/content/india-wants-join-nonproliferation-treaty).

51. PTI, ‘Modi may use military option if terror attack traced to Pakistan’. Hindu Bus. Line (2015), (available at http://www.thehindubusinessline.com/news/modi-may-use-military-option-if-terrorattack-traced-to-pakistan/article6864786.ece).

Chapter 5: Command and Control of India's Nuclear Arsenal. Lauren J. Borja & M.V. Ramana

Acton, J. M. 2018. "Escalation through Entanglement: How the Vulnerability of Command-andControl Systems Raises the Risks of an Inadvertent Nuclear War." International Security 43 (1):56–99. doi:10.1162/isec_a_00320.

AFP. 2005. "US Unveils Plans to Make India 'Major World Power." Agence France-Presse, March 26, 2005.

Airforce Technology. n.d. "GSAT-7A: A Military Communications Satellite Developed by ISRO for IAF." Accessed 21 June 2019. https://www.airforce-technology.com/projects/gsat-7a/

Annual Report 2015-2016. 2016. "Bharat Electronics." Bangalore, India. http://www.bel-india.in/Documentviews.aspx?fileName=Annual%20Report%202015-16.pdf

Annual Report 2017-2018. 2018. Bharat Electronics.Bangalore, India: http://www.bel-india.in/Documentviews.aspx?fileName=annual-report-2017-18-28918.pdf

Arbatov, A., V. Dvorkin, P. Topychkanov, T. Zhao, and L. Bin. 2017. "Entanglement: Chinese and Russian Perspectives on Non-Nuclear Weapons and Nuclear Risks." Washington, D.C.:Carnegie Endowment for International Peace. https://carnegieendowment.org/2017/11/08/entanglement-chinese-and-russian-perspectives-on-non-nuclear-weapons-and-nuclear-riskspub-73162

Bagchi, I. 2013. "Even a Midget Nuke Strike Will Lead to Massive Retaliation, India Warns Pak.The Times of India, April 30, 2013. http://timesofindia.indiatimes.com/articleshow/19793847.cms?utm_source=contentofinterest&utm_medium=text&utm_campaign=cppst

Bagla, P. 2018. "Agni 5 Missile That Can Strike China Set To Enter India's Arsenal." NDTV.Com,January 19, 2018. https://www.ndtv.com/india-news/agni-5-missile-that-can-strike-china-setto-enter-indias-arsenal-1802188

Bhatia, V. K., Air Marshal (Retd). 2010. "AFNET Kick-Starts." SP's Aviation, October 2010. http://www.sps-aviation.com/story/?id=582

Bhatia, V. K., Air Marshal (Retd). 2012. "Raytheon's Project Athena Multi-Domain Awareness System." SP's Aviation, May 2012. http://search.proquest.com/docview/1017859991/abstract/774599C9FFAB4267PQ/1

Blair, B. 1985. Strategic Command and Control. 1st ed. Washington, D.C: Brookings Institution Press.

Bracken, P. 2016. "The Cyber Threat to Nuclear Stability." Orbis 60 (2): 188–203. doi:10.1016/j.orbis.2016.02.002.

Bush, G. W. 2004. "Next Steps in Strategic Partnership with India." U.S. Department Of State Archive. January 12, 2004. https://2001-2009.state.gov/p/sca/rls/pr/28109.htm

Carter, A. 1987. Managing Nuclear Operations. Washington, D.C: Brookings Institution Press.

Chakraborty, A. 2018. "12 Missions, 12 Months - ISRO's Mega Plan For 2018 Revealed. Details Here." NDTV, April 16, 2018. https://www.ndtv.com/india-news/isro-missions-2018-12-launches-12-months-isros-mega-plan-for-2018-revealed-details-here-1838144

Chengappa, R. 1998. "Dangerous Nuclear Mishaps Loom Large; Defined Command, Control Structure Needed." India Today, July 13, 1998. https://www.indiatoday.in/magazine/defence/story/19980713-dangerous-nuclear-mishaps-loom-large-defined-command-control-structureneeded-828095-1998-07-13

Chengappa, R. 2000. Weapons of Peace: The Secret Story of India's Quest to Be a Nuclear Power. New Delhi: Harper Collins.

Clary, C., and V. Narang. 2019. "India's Counterforce Temptations: Strategic Dilemmas, Doctrine,and Capabilities." International Security 43 (3): 7–52. doi:10.1162/isec_a_00340.

Cohen, S. P., and S. Dasgupta. 2012. Arming without Aiming: India's Military Modernization. 2 edition ed. Washington, DC: Brookings Institution Press.

DAE. 1998. "Press Conference." Globalsecurity.Org. May 16, 1998. https://www.globalsecurity.org/wmd/library/news/india/1998/980500-conf.htm

European Space Agency. 2018. "Satellite Frequency Bands." European Space Agency. October 3, 2018. https://www.esa.int/Our_Activities/Telecommunications_Integrated_Applications/Satellite_frequency_bands

Fairchild Space Company. 1986. "Survivability Enhancement Study for C3I/BM Ground Segments." DOE/SF/15929-1. San Francisco: U.S. Department of Energy. https://www.osti.gov/servlets/purl/6588985

Gershman, J., and Z. Mian. 2005. "A Story of Leaders, Partners, and Clients." Washington, D. C.:Institute for Policy Studies. https://ips-dc.org/a_story_of_leaders_partners_and_clients/

Green Pine Radar (Israel). 2018. "Missile Defense Advocacy Alliance (Blog)." December 2018.http://missiledefenseadvocacy.org/missile-defense-systems-2/allied-air-and-missile-defense-systems/allied-sensor-systems/green-pine-radar-elm-2080-israel/

Hull, J. A. 1987. "NSEP Fiber Optics System Study, Background Report: Nuclear Effects on FiberOptic Transmission Systems." NTIA Report 87-227. Washington, D.C.: U.S. Department of Commerce. https://

cryptome.org/2012/09/ntia-87-227.pdf 16 L. J. BORJA AND M. V. RAMANA

Hull, T. 2018. "Air Force Space Command Supply Chain Risk Management of Strategic Capabilities DODIG-2018-143." https://media.defense.gov/2018/Aug/16/2001955109/-1/-1/1/DODIG-2018-143_REDACTED.PDF

India Strategic. 2018. "Air Officer Commanding In Chief, Central Air Command, Inaugurated,"August 2018. https://www.indiastrategic.in/2018/08/03/air-officer-commanding-in-chief-central-air-command-inaugurated/

India Today Web Desk. 2019. "Isro Successfully Launches CARTO-SAT-3, 13 Nano-Satellites from Sriharikota." India Today, November 27, 2019. https://www.indiatoday.in/science/story/isrolaunches-earth-imaging-satellite-cartosat-3-13-nano-satellites-from-1622889-2019-11-27

Indian Navy. 2019. "Naval Commanders' at Kochi for Operational Discussions." March 17, 2019. https://www.indiannavy.nic.in/content/naval-commanders-kochi-operational-discussions

Indian PSLV Launches RISAT-2BR1 Military Satellite. 2019. NASASpaceFlight.Com (blog). December 11, 2019. https://www.nasaspaceflight.com/2019/12/indian-pslv-launch-risat-2br1-military-satellite/IndraStra Global Editorial Team. 2015. "ANALYSIS | India's Integrated Air Command & Control System (IACCS) : A NCW Milestone." IndraStra, September 28, 2015. https://www.indrastra.com/2015/09/ANALYSIS-IACCS-257.html

Joshi, Y. 2019. "Angles and Dangles: Arihant and the Dilemma of India's Undersea Nuclear eapons". War on the Rocks. January 14, 2019. https://warontherocks.com/2019/01/anglesand-dangles-arihant-and-the-dilemma-of-indias-undersea-nuclear-weapons/Kampani, G. 1998. "From Existential to Minimum Deterrence: Explaining India's Decision to Test." The Nonproliferation Review 6 (1): 12–24. doi:10.1080/10736709808436732.

Kampani, G. 2014. "New Delhi's Long Nuclear Journey." International Security 38 (4): 79–114. doi:10.1162/ISEC_a_00158.

Kampani, G. 2016. "India's Evolving Civil-military Institutions in an Operational Nuclear Context." Carnegie Endowment. https://carnegieendowment.org/2016/06/30/india-s-evolvingcivil-military-institutions-in-operational-nuclear-context-pub-63910.

Karnad, B. 2002. "India's Force Planning Imperative: The Thermonuclear Option." In Nuclear India in the Twenty-First Century, edited by D. R. SarDesai and R. G. C. Thomas. New York:Palgrave. doi:10.1057/9780230109230_5.

Karnad, B. 2008. India's Nuclear Policy. Westport, Conn: Praeger.

Karnad, B. 2017. "Why Concerns about an India-Pakistan Nuclear War are Highly Exaggerated."Hindustan Times, March 30, 2017. http://www.hindustantimes.com/analysis/concerns-about-anindia-pakistan-nuclear-war-are-highly-exaggerated/story-rnKGeo-3qZ0oCpMhR1edRqL.html

Khosla, L. 1981. "Use of Nuclear Weapons." IDSA Journal XIII 4: 463–478.

Koithara, V. 2012. Managing India's Nuclear Forces. 1 Edition. Washington, D.C: Brookings Institution Press.

Kristensen, H. M., and M. Korda. 2018. "Indian Nuclear Forces, 2018." Bulletin of the Atomic Scientists 74 (6): 361–366. doi:10.1080/009 63402.2018.1533162.

Kukreja, A., and M. Dhiraj. 2015. "Integrated Air Defence for the Indian Airspace." Indian Defence Review, January 29, 2015. http://www.indiandefencereview.com/news/integrated-air-defencefor-the-indian-airspace/

Kumar, C. 2019a. "Isro Satellites Can Map 87% Land Area of Pakistan, in HD." The Times of India,February 28, 2019. https://timesofindia.indiatimes.com/india/isro-satellites-can-map-87-landarea-of-pakistan-in-hd/articleshow/68196974.cms

Kumar, C. 2019b. "Days after A-SAT, EMISAT Adds to India's Defence Capability." The Times of India, April 1, 2019. https://timesofindia.indiatimes.com/india/days-after-a-sat-emisat-add-toindias-defence-capability/articleshow/68669542.cms

Kumar, R. 2006. Indian Nuclear Command and Control Dilemma. Masters, Monterrey, CA: Naval Postgraduate School. https://calhoun.nps.edu/handle/10945/2639

Lt, K., and P. C. General (Retd). 2018. "Army's Battlefield Management System — Dumped?" SP's

Land Forces, January 8, 2018. http://www.spslandforces.com/experts-speak/?id=326&h=Armys-Battlefield-Management-System-Dumped

Madhumathi, D. S. 2017. "India Gets a Sharper Eye in the Sky with ISRO's Cartosat-2E." The Hindu, June 29, 2017. https://www.the-hindu.com/sci-tech/science/india-gets-a-sharper-eye-inthe-sky/article19180628.ece

Mahesh, K. 2017. "Navy to Reach Ships and Subs from Pudur." The Times of India, December 26,2017. https://timesofindia.indiatimes.com/city/hyderabad/navy-to-reach-ships-and-subs-frompudur/article-show/62261258.cms

Mian, Z., M. V. Ramana, and A. H. Nayyar. 2019. "Nuclear Submarines in South Asia: New Risks and Dangers." Journal for Peace and Nuclear Disarmament: 1–19. doi:10.1080/25751654.2019.1621425.

Nagal, B. S., Lt Gen (retd). 2014. "Nuclear No First Use Policy." Force National Security and Aerospace Newsmagazine, December 2014. http://forceindia.net/guest-column/guest-columnb-s-nagal/nucle-ar-no-first-use-policy/

Narang, V. 2013. "Five Myths about India's Nuclear Posture." The Washing-ton Quarterly 36 (3):143–157. doi:10.1080/0163660X.2013.825555.

NCTA- The Internet & Television Association. 2018. "Average U.S. In-ternet Speeds More Than Double Global Average," July 27, 2018. /whats-new/average-us-internet-speeds-more-doubleglobal-aver-age

NSAB. 1999. "Draft Report of National Security Advisory Board on In-dian Nuclear Doctrine."New Delhi: National Security Advisory Board. http://mea.gov.in/in-focus-article.htm?18916/Draft+Repor t+of+National+Security+Advisory+Board+on+Indian+Nuclear+ Doctrine

Pandit, R. 2004. "First Chief to Retire, but Where's Infrastructure?" The Times of India, June 2,2004.

Pandit, R. 2008. "Army for Tunnels to Protect Troops: Wants Shield against Nuke & Biological Warfare along Disputed Pak, China Bor-ders." The Times of India, November 1, 2008.

Pandit, R. 2012a. "Defence Fortifies Western Front, New Bas-es along Pakistan Border." The Economic Times, July 31, 2012. http://search.proquest.com/docview/1030138690/abstract/2AB1432D72AD46CAPQ/1

Pandit, R. 2012b. "India Boring Border Tunnels to Take on China, Paki-stan." The Times of India, August 15, 2012. https://timesofindia.indiatimes.com/india/India-boring-border-tunnels-totake-on-China-Pakistan/articleshow/15509722.cms

Pandit, R. 2014a. "Navy Kicks off Largest Combat Exercise with Dedicated Satellite Above." The Times of India, February 13, 2014. https://timesofindia.indiatimes.com/india/Navy-kicks-offlargest-combat-exercise-with-dedicated-satellite-above/articleshow/30349037.cms

Pandit, R. 2014b. "Navy Gets New Facility to Communicate with Nuclear Submarines Prowling Underwater." The Times of India, July 31, 2014. https://timesofindia.indiatimes.com/india/

Navy-gets-new-facility-to-communicate-with-nuclear-submarines-prowling-underwater/arti cleshow/39371121.cms

Pandit, R. 2014c. "Naval Intelligence Network Launch Tomorrow." The Times of India, November 21, 2014. https://timesofindia.indiatimes.com/india/Naval-intelligence-network-launch-tomor row/articleshow/45237364.cms

Pandit, R. 2015. "India to Plug Holes in Sky with Web of Radars." The Times of India, June 20, 2015. https://timesofindia.indiatimes.com/india/India-to-plug-holes-in-sky-with-web-fradars/articleshow/47752076.cms

Pandit, R. 2019. "India's Military Brass Wants Swifter Build-up of Border Infrastructure with China." The Times of India, April 14, 2019. https://timesofindia.indiatimes.com/india/indiasmilitary-brass-wants-swifter-build-up-of-border-infrastructure-with-china/articleshow/68879141.cms

Perkovich, G. 1999. India's Nuclear Bomb: The Impact on Global Proliferation. Berkeley: University of California Press.

Prime Minister's Office. 2003. "Cabinet Committee on Security Reviews Progress in Operationalizing India's Nuclear Doctrine." New Delhi: Government of India. http://pib.nic.in/archieve/lreleng/lyr2003/rjan2003/04012003/r040120033.html

PSLV-C46/RISAT-2B MISSION. 2019. "Launch Kit." Bengaluru, India: Indian Space Research Organization. https://www.isro.gov.in/pslv-c46-mission/launch-kit 18 L. J. BORJA AND M. V. RAMANA

PTI. 2009. "India to Launch Spy Satellite on April 20." The Times of India, April 8, 2009. https://timesofindia.indiatimes.com/india/India-to-launch-spy-satellite-on-April-20/articleshow/4374544.cms

Pubby, M. 2009. "India in N-Sub Club,Arihant to Be Inducted in Next 2 Yrs." The Indian Express,

July 26, 2009. https://indianexpress.com/article/india/latest-news/india-in-nsub-club-arihantto-be-nducted-in-next-2-yrs/

Raghuvanshi, V. 2015. "Challenges Await Completion of Indian AF Net-Centric System." Defense News, October 10, 2015. https://www.defensenews.com/air/2015/10/10/challenges-await-com   pletion-of-indian-af-net-centric-system/

Raghuvanshi, V. 2020. "New Weapons Purchases Suffer under India's Latest Defense Budget." Defense News, February 4, 2020, sec. Asia Pacific. https://www.defensenews.com/global/asiapacific/2020/02/04/new-weapons-purchases-suffer-under-indias-latest-defense-budget/

Raj, N. G. 2013. "ISRO Plans a New High-Resolution Earth Satellite." The Hindu, March 6, 2013, sec. Science. https://www.thehindu.com/sci-tech/science/isro-plans-a-new-highresolutionearth-satellite/article4482404.ece

Rajagopalan, R. P., and N. Prasad. 2017. Space India 2.0: Commerce, Policy, Security and Governance Perspectives. New Delhi: Observer Research Foundation.

Ramana, M. V. 2009. "India's Nuclear Enclave and the Practice of Secrecy." In Nuclear Power and Atomic Publics: Society and Culture in India and Pakistan, edited by I. Abraham, 41–67.Bloomington: Indiana University Press.

Ramana, M. V., and L. J. Borja. 2020. "The Computer Infection of Kudankulam and Its Implications." India Forum, January 10, 2020. https://www.theindiaforum.in/article/computer-infection-kudankulam-and-its-implications

Ramesh, S. 2018a. "The Militaristic Claims of ISRO's Latest Satellite Have Been Greatly Exaggerated." ThePrint, December 4, 2018. https://theprint.in/science/the-militaristic-claimsof-isros-latest-satellite-have-been-greatly-exaggerated/158545/

Ramesh, S. 2018b. "ISRO to Launch Advanced GSAT-7A Satellite for IAF and Army Today."ThePrint, December 18, 2018. https://theprint.in/science/isro-to-launch-advanced-gsat-7a-satellite-for-iaf-and-army-today/165548/

Riedel, B. 2002. "American Diplomacy and the 1999 Kargil Summit at Blair House." Center for the Advanced Study of India, University of Pennsylvania.

RISAT 2B, 2BR1, 2BR2. 2020. "Guenter's Space Page." January 13, 2020. https://space.skyrocket.de/doc_sdat/risat-2b.htm

Rohit, T. K. 2018. "GSAT-7A, ISRO's 'Angry Bird', Takes to the Skies." The Hindu, December 19,2018, sec. Science. https://www.the-hindu.com/sci-tech/science/isro-successfully-launches-gsat7a/article25781226.ece

Saran, S. 2013a. "Is India's Nuclear Deterrent Credible?" presented at the India Habitat Centre, New Delhi, April 24. http://www.armscontrolwonk.com/files/2013/05/Final-Is-Indias-NuclearDeterrent-Credible-rev1-2-1-3.pdf

Saran, S. 2013b. "Weapon that Has More than Symbolic Value." The Hindu, May 4, 2013.

Shaheen, S. 2019. Nuclear Command and Control Norms: A Comparative Study. 1st ed. New York:Routledge. https://www.routledge.com/Nuclear-Command-and-Control-Norms-AComparative-Study-1st-Edition/Shaheen/p/book/9781138349292

Sidhu, W. P. S. 2013. "Whose Finger on the Nuclear Trigger at Sea?" Livemint, August 4, 2013. https://www.livemint.com/Opinion/FesGy-5sItj3WTJywQdfiKO/Whose-finger-on-the-nucleartrigger-at-sea.html

Singh, S. 2018. "Isro to Launch Hyperspectral Imaging Sat with 30 Foreign Satellites on Nov 29."The Times of India, November 26, 2018. https://timesofindia.indiatimes.com/india/isro-tolaunch-hyper-spectral-imaging-sat-with-30-foreign-satellites-on-nov-29/articleshow/66801810.cms

Singh, S. 2019a. "Isro Satellite that Could Have Scanned JeM Camp after Bombing." The Times of India, March 6, 2019. https://timesofindia.indiatimes.com/india/risat-2-that-can-see-throughclouds-could-have-scanned-jem-camp-after-bombing/articleshow/68294290.cms

Singh, S. 2019b. "Hi-Tech Antenna of Risat-2B, Developed in Record 13 Months by Isro, Deployed." The Times of India, May 22, 2019. https://timesofindia.indiatimes.com/india/hitech-antenna-of-risat-2b-developed-in-record-13-months-by-isro-deployed/articleshow/69453184.cms

Singh, S. 2019c. "Isro to Launch Another 'Eye in the Sky' Risat-2BR1 on December 11, Will Help Boost Border Surveillance." The Times of India, December 3, 2019. https://timesofindia.indiatimes.com/india/isro-to-launch-another-eye-in-the-sky-risat-2br1-on-dec-11-will-help-boostborder-surveillance/articleshow/72340281.cms

Special Correspondent. 2017. "India to Be Second Country to Use ELF Facility." The Hindu, May 20, 2017. https://www.thehindu.com/news/cities/Hyderabad/india-to-be-second-country-touse-elf-facility/article18517424.ece

Subramanian, A. P. 2015. Agni V: Incremental Capability Addition. New Delhi: Centre for Air Power Studies. http://capsindia.org/files/documents/CAPS_Infocus_AS_12.pdf

Sundaram, K., and M. V. Ramana. 2018. "India and the Policy of No First Use of Nuclear Weapons." Journal for Peace and Nuclear Disarmament 1 (1): 152–168. doi:10.1080/25751654.2018.1438737.

Sundarji, G. K. 1984. "Strategy in the Age of Nuclear Deterrence and Its Application to Developing Countries." Simla: Unpublished Manuscript.

Talmadge, C. 2017. "Would China Go Nuclear? Assessing the Risk of Chinese Nuclear Escalation in a Conventional War with the United States." International Security 41 (4): 50–92.doi:10.1162/ISEC_a_00274.

Tejonmayam, U. 2018. "Isro Releases Images Captured by Microsat and Nanosatellite." The Times of India, January 23, 2018. https://timesofindia.indiatimes.com/home/science/isro-releasesimages-captured-by-microsat-and-nanosatellite/articleshow/62622667.cms

Tellis, A. 2001. India's Emerging Nuclear Posture. Santa Monica: Rand.

TNN. 2008. "IAF Plan to Link Civilian, Defence Radars Takes Off." The Economic Times, December 20, 2008. https://economictimes.indiatimes.com/iaf-plan-to-link-civilian-defenceradars-takes-off/articleshow/3865728.cms?from=mdr

TNN. 2015. "Nod for Rs 8,000 Crore Air Force Radar System." The Times of India, September 23, 2015. https://timesofindia.indiatimes.com/india/Nod-for-Rs-8000-crore-Air-Force-radar-system/articleshow/49083074.cms

UCS Satellite Database." n.d. "Union of Concerned Scientists." Accessed July 9, 2019. https://www. ucsusa.org/nuclear-weapons/space-weapons/satellite-database

Unnithan, S. 2018. "INS Arihant Returned Yesterday from 20-Day Deterrent Patrol." India Today, November 5, 2018. https://www.india-today.in/india/story/ins-arihant-returned-yesterdayfrom-20-day-deterrent-patrol-1383188-2018-11-05

White, R. B. 2014. "Command and Control of India's Nuclear Forces." The Nonproliferation Review 21 (3–4): 261–274. doi:10.1080/1073 6700.2014.1072994.

Wueger, D. 2016. "India's Nuclear-Armed Submarines: Deterrence or Danger?" Washington Quarterly 39 (3): 77–90. doi:10.1080/0163 660X.2016.1232636.

Yadav, Y. 2017. "Hackers from China Break into Secret Indian Government Video Chat." The New Indian Express, November 19, 2017. https://www.newindianexpress.com/nation/2017/nov/19/hackers-from-china-break-into-secret-indian-government-video-chat-1705010.html

Yarynich, V. E. 2003. C3: Nuclear Command, Control, Cooperation. Washington, D.C.: Center for Defense Information.

Chapter 6: The Twenty Years' Crisis of Nuclear South Asia, 1998–2018: A Workshop Report. Zia Mian a, A. H. Nayyara and M. V. Ramana b

1. Speech by Prime Minister Atal Bihari Vajpayee, United Nations, 24 September 1998. http://www.acronym.org.uk/old/ archive/spsep98.htm

2. Speeches by Prime Minister Nawaz Sharif, United Nations, 23 September 1998. http://www.acronym.org.uk/old/archive/ spsep98.htm

3. "Security Council Condemns Nuclear Tests by India and Pakistan," 6 June 1998. https://www.un.org/press/en/1998/ sc6528.doc.htm

References

Kothari, S., and Z. Mian, eds. 2003. Out of the Nuclear Shadow, Revised and Updated. 2nd ed. Karachi: Oxford University Press.

Kristensen, H. M., and R. S. Norris. 2013. "Global Nuclear Weapons Inventories, 1945–2013." Bulletin of the Atomic Scientists 69 (5): 75–81. doi:10.1177/0096340213501363.

Kristensen, H. M., and R. S. Norris. 2018. "Status of World Nuclear Forces," June 2018. Federation of American Scientists. https://fas.org/issues/nuclear-weapons/status-worldnuclear-forces

Ramana, M. V., and C. R. Reddy. 2003. *Prisoners of the Nuclear Dream*. Hyderabad: Orient Longman

Chapter 7: India-Pakistan Crises under the Nuclear Shadow: The Role of Reassurance. Karthika Sasikumar

Abbas, Z. 2008. "A Hoax Call That Could Have Triggered War." Dawn, December 6. Accessed 20 June 2011. http://archives.dawn.com/2008/12/06/top2.htm

Anon. 1999. "Indian Navy Fully Prepared to Counter N-Strikes." Times of India. Bombay, June 7. 8.

Anon. 2001. "War against Terrorism Will Be Fought Decisively: P.M." India Info, December 13. newsarchives.indiainfo.com/spotlight/parliament/13pm4.html

Anon. 2002. "'Every Country Has the Right to Pre-Emptive Strikes": Jaswant Singh." Indian Express, September 30.

Anon. 2003. "Pak Fitter Case for Pre-Emptive Strike: Sinha." Times of India, April 9. Accessed 11 July 2011. http://articles.timesofindia.indiatimes.com/2003-04-09/india/27265639_1_crossborder-terrorism-fitter-case-emptive

Anon. 2006. "Talks with Pak Not on Agenda Now: India." Indian Express, July 15. Accessed 6 January 2012. http://www.expressindia.com/news/fullstory.php?newsid=71124 doi:10.1094/ PDIS-11-11-0999-PDN

Anon. 2014. "If Modi Becomes P.M., Pak Intruders Won't Dare to Cross Border: Amit Shah." Indian Express, April 23. Accessed 27 March 2018. http://indianexpress.com/article/india/politics/if-modi-becomes-pm-pak-intruders-wont-dare-to-cross-border-amit-shah/

Anon. 2016a. "India's Surgical Strikes across LoC: Full Statement by DGMO Lt. Gen Ranbir Singh." Hindustan Times, September 29. Accessed 27 March 2018. https://www.hindustantimes.com/india-news/india-s-surgical-strikes-across-loc-full-statement-by-dgmo-lt-genranbir-singh/story-Q5yrp0gjvxKPGazDzAnVsM.html

Anon. 2016b. "Converting LoC into International Border 'Only Option' with India, Pakistan: Natwar Singh." Daily News and Analysis India, September 25. Accessed 3 January 2018. http://www.dnaindia.com/india/report-converting-loc-into-international-border-only-option-withindia-pakistan-natwar-singh-2258480

Anon. 2016c. "Nuclear War with Pakistan: I.A.S. Officer Runs Twitter Poll, Says Pakistanis Voted 'No, Life is Too Precious.'" Indian Express, September 19. Accessed 26 March 2018. http://indianexpress.com/article/india/india-news-india/ur-attack-pakistan-india-nuclear-war-iasofficer-sanjay-dixit-3039280/

Anon. 2018. "War of Words Breaks Out Over Surgical Strikes." Hindu, June 29. Accessed 7 May 2019. https://www.thehindu.com/todays-paper/tp-national/war-of-words-over-surgical-strikes/article24284321.ece

Bell, M. S., and J. M. Macdonald. 2019. "How to Think about Nuclear Crises." Texas National Security Review, February. Accessed 7 May 2019. https://tnsr.org/2019/03/how-to-think-about-nuclear-crises/

Betts, R. 1987. Nuclear Blackmail and Nuclear Balance. Washington DC: Brookings Institution. Carson, A. 2016. "Facing Off and Saving Face: Covert Intervention and Escalation Management in the Korean War." International Organization 70: 103–131. doi:10.1017/S00208818315000284.

Chinna, M. A. S. 2018. "Surgical Strike Overhype Did Not Help, Says General Who Oversaw Operations." Indian Express, December 8. Accessed 16 December 2018. https://indianexpress.com/article/india/surgical-strike-overhype-did-not-help-says-general-d-s-hooda-who-oversaw-operations-5483929/

Coll, S. 2009. "The Back Channel." New Yorker, March 2.

Das, S., and E. Roche. 2017. "Beheading of Soldiers: India Sends Warning to Pakistan." LiveMint, May 3. Accessed 15 July 2018. https://www.livemint.com/Politics/Aj9G5NIZSUYJvJHCbfFE4H/Beheading-of-soldiers-India-sends-warning-to-Pakistan.html

Datta, S. 2005. "'Threat of Nuclear War in Kargil Was a Bogey.'" Outlook, March 7.

Dugger, C. W. 2002. "The World: Unthinkable; Eyeball to Eyeball, and Blinking in Denial." New York Times, June 2. Accessed 16 May 2018. https://www.nytimes.com/2002/06/02/weekinreview/the-world-unthinkable-eyeball-to-eyeball-and-blinking-in-denial.html

Dulat, A. S., and A. Durrani. 2011. "India–Pakistan: Need for Intelligence Cooperation." Hindu, July 14. Accessed 10 July 2018. https://www.thehindu.com/opinion/op-ed/indiapakistan-needfor-intelligence-cooperation/article2224644.ece

Dulat, A. S., A. Durrani, and A. Sinha. 2018. The Spy Chronicles: RAW, ISI and the Illusion of Peace. New Delhi: HarperCollins.

Fuhrmann, M., and T. Sechser. 2013. "Crisis Bargaining and Nuclear Blackmail." International Organization 67: 173–195. doi:10.1017/S0020818312000392.

Ganguly, S. 1995. "Indo-Pakistani Nuclear Issues and the Stability/Instability Paradox." Studies in Conflict and Terrorism 18: 325–334. doi:10.1080/10576109508435989.

Gardiner, S. 2002. "A Nuclear War between India and Pakistan is Likely." Washington Post, January 20.

Gokhale, N. 2017. Securing India the Modi Way: Pathankot, Surgical Strikes and More. New Delhi: Bloomsbury India.

Guha, S. 1999. "India Aims to Be a Stabilising Power in Region." Times of India, July 25.

Hagerty, D. 2008. "The Implications of a Nuclear-Armed Iran in Light of South Asia's Nuclear Experience." In Nuclear Proliferation in South Asia: Crisis Behaviour and the Bomb, edited by S. Ganguly and S. P. Kapur, 212–242. London: Routledge.

Hayes, J. 2009. "Identity and Securitization in the Democratic Peace: The United States and the Divergence of Response to India and Iran's Nuclear Programs." International Studies Quarterly 53 (4): 977–999. doi:10.1111/j.1468-2478.2009.00565.x.

Hoodbhoy, P. 2013. "Pakistan: Climbing the Nuclear Ladder." In Confronting the Bomb: Pakistani and Indian Scientists Speak Out, edited by P. Hoodbhoy, 68–89. Karachi: Oxford University Press.

Howard, M. 1982–1983. "Reassurance and Deterrence: Western Defense in the 1980s." Foreign Affairs 61 (2): 309–324. doi:10.2307/20041437.

Joshi, M. 1999. "The ABCs (and Whys) of India's 'N-Doctrine.'" Times of India, August 22. Kampani, G. 2002. India's Compellance Strategy: Calling Pakistan's Nuclear Bluff over Kashmir.

Monterey: Monterey Institute of International Studies. March. Kapur, S. 2018. "From Copenhagen to Uri and across the Line of Control: India's 'Surgical Strikes' as a Case of Securitisation in Two Acts." Global Discourse 8 (1): 62–79. doi:10.1080/23269995.2017.1406633.

Kapur, S. P. 2006. Dangerous Deterrent: Nuclear Weapons Proliferation and Conflict in South Asia. Stanford: Stanford University Press.

Karnad, B. 2002. "A New Strategy for the LoC and Low-Intensity Warfare in Kashmir." In The Global Threat of Terror: Ideological, Material and Political Linkages, edited by K. Gill and A. Sahni, 141–160. New Delhi: Bulwark Books for the Institute of Conflict Management.

Kumar, D. 1999. "Secret Tapes Bare Pakistan's Game Plan in Kargil." Times of India, June 12. Ladwig, W. C., III. 2007–2008. "A Cold Start for Hot Wars?" International Security 32 (3):158–190. doi:10.1162/isec.2008.32.3.158.

Lavoy, P. R. 2009. Asymmetric Warfare in South Asia: The Causes and Consequences of the Kargil Conflict. Cambridge and New York: Cambridge University Press.

Manchanda, R. 2001. "Covering Kargil: South Asia's First 'Media War.'" In Kargil and After: Challenges for Indian Policy, edited by K. Bajpai, A. Karim, and A. Mattoo, 74–90. New Delhi:Har-Anand.

Marcus, J. 2000. "Analysis: The World's Most Dangerous Place?" BBC, March 23. Accessed 9 July 2018. http://news.bbc.co.uk/2/hi/south_asia/687021.stm

Mehta, G. A., (retd.). 2003. "India Was on Brink of War Twice" Rediff, January 2. Accessed 23 January 2005. http://www.rediff.com/news/2003/jan/02ashok.htm

Montgomery, E. B. 2006. "Breaking Out of the Security Dilemma: Realism, Reassurance, and the Problem of Uncertainty." International Security 31 (2): 151–185. doi:10.1162/isec.2006.31.2.151.

Narang, V. 2009. "Playing Chicken without a Wheel (Or a P.A.L.): Pakistan's past and Evolving Nuclear Posture." Cambridge MA: Department of Government, Harvard University.Unpublished Working Paper.

Narang, V. 2010. "Posturing for Peace?: The Sources and Deterrence Consequences of Regional Power Nuclear Postures." Ph.D., Department of Government, Harvard University, Cambridge,MA.

Narang, V. 2014. Nuclear Strategy in the Modern Era: Regional Powers and International Conflict.Princeton, NJ: Princeton University Press.

Narang, V. 2018. "India's Nuclear Strategy Twenty Years Later: From Reluctance to Maturation." India Review 17 (1): 159–179. doi:10.1080/14736489.2018.1415289.

Narang, V., and C. Clary. 2016. "Confusion is Risky." Indian Express, November 18. Accessed 9 June 2018. http://indianexpress.com/article/opinion/columns/manohar-parrikar-nuclearpolicy-no-first-use-nfu-atal-bihari-vajpayee-confusion-4381028/

Nayak, P., and M. Krepon. 2012. The Unfinished Crisis: U.S. Crisis Management after the 2008 Mumbai Attacks. Washington D.C.: Henry L. Stimson Center. February.

Nolan, J. E. 2000. "Preparing for the 2001 Nuclear Posture Review." Arms Control Today 30 (9): 10–14.

Pande, A. 2005. "South Asia: Counter-Terrorism Policies and Postures after 9/11." Faultlines (15). http://www.satp.org/satporgtp/publication/faultlines/volume15/Article4.htm#1

Pegahi, T. N. 2018. "Nuclear Weapons Did Not Embolden Pakistan: Drawing the Right Lessons for North Korea." warontherocks. com, January 22. Accessed 10 May 2018. https://warontherocks. com/2018/01/nuclear-weapons-not-embolden-pakistan-drawing-right-lessons-northkorea/Peri, D. 2016. "J.E.M Hand Seen in Uri Attack; D.G.M.O. Calls Pak Counterpart." Hindu, November 1. Accessed 26 March 2018. http://www.thehindu.com/news/national/other-states/JeM-hand-seen-in-Uri-attack-DGMO-calls-Pak-counterpart/article14986871.ece

Pugwash Conferences on Science and World Affairs. 2002. "Report on Nuclear Safety, Nuclear Stability and Nuclear Strategy in Pakistan: A Concise Report of A Visit by Landau Network –Centro Volta." Vol.: Pugwash Conferences on Science and World Affairs. https://pugwash.org/2002/01/14/report-on-nuclear-safety-nuclear-stability-and-nuclear-strategy-in-pakistan/

Rabasa, A., R. Blackwill, P. Chalk, K. Cragin, C. C. Fair, B. A. Jackson, B. M. Jenkins, S. G. Jones, N. Shestak, and A. Tellis. 2009. "The Lessons of Mumbai." Occasional Paper 249. Santa Monica, CA: RAND Corporation.

Raghavan, S., and R. Chaudhuri. 2008. "Unlimited Damage." Daily News and Analysis India, December 30. Accessed 4 January 2018. http://www.dnaindia.com/analysis/main-articleunlimited-damage-1217693

Raghavan, V. R. 2004. "The Double-Edged Effect in South Asia." Washington Quarterly 27 (4): 147–155. doi:10.1162/wash.2004.27.4.147.

Rajagopalan, R. 2008. "India: The Logic of Assured Retaliation." In The Long Shadow: Nuclear Weapons and Security in 21st Century Asia, edited by M. Alagappa, 188. Stanford: Stanford University Press.

Ramana, M. V. 2003. "Risks of a LOW Doctrine." Economic and Political Weekly, March 1.

Riedel, B. 2002, "American Diplomacy and the 1999 Summit at Blair House." Center for the Advanced Study of India, University of Pennsylvania. Accessed 21 May 2002. http://www.sas.upenn.edu/casi/reports/RiedelPaper051302.htm

Roy Choudhury, R. 2004. "Nuclear Doctrine, Declaratory Policy, and Escalation Control." April 27. Washington DC: Henry L. Stimson Center. https://www.stimson.org/content/nucleardoctrine-declaratory-policy-and-escalation-control Roychowdhury, S., and J. Singh. 1999. "Should India Cross the LoC in Kargil?" Times of India, June 20.

Sagan, S., and K. Waltz. 2003. "Indian and Pakistani Nuclear Weapons: For Better or for Worse." In The Spread of Nuclear Weapons: Debate Renewed, edited by S. Sagan and K. Waltz, 88–124.New York and London: W.W. Norton.

Samanta, P. D. 2010. "26/11: How India Debated a War with Pakistan that November." Indian Express, November 26. Accessed 29 November 2010. http://www.indianexpress.com/news/26-11-how-india-debated-a-war-with-pakistan-that-november/716240/0

Sardesai, D. R. 2003. Globalization is Having Positive Effects in India, Scholars Conclude at UCLA Conference. Los Angeles: UCLA. https://www.international.ucla.edu/article.asp?parentid=3877&parentid=3877

Sasikumar, K. 2007. "India's Emergence as a 'Responsible' Nuclear Power." International Journal 62 (4): 825–844. doi:10.1177/002070200706200407.

Sharma, P. 2013. "News of a Beheading." Outlook, January 28. Accessed 15 July 2018. https://www.outlookindia.com/magazine/story/news-of-a-beheading/283602

Shukla, A. 2017. "Speculation in Washington about Nuclear Doctrinal Changes by India."Business Standard, March 22. Accessed 27 March 2018. http://www.business-standard.com/article/current-affairs/speculation-in-washington-about-nuclear-doctrinal-changes-by-india-117032101292_1.html

Sidhu, W. P. S. 2007. "Operation Vijay and Operation Parakram: The Victory of Theory?" In The India–Pakistan Nuclear Relationship, edited by E. Sridharan, 207–238. New Delhi: Routledge.

Singh, J. 2007. In Service of Emergent India: A Call to Honor. Bloomington, IN: Indiana University Press.

Singh, R., and P. P. Chaudhuri. 2011. "Can India Pull Off a Covert Strike?" Hindustan Times, May 6. Accessed 16 December 2018. https://www.hindustantimes.com/delhi-news/can-indiapull-off-a-covert-strike/story-yeeFCRlawj1KUPugz6b05K.html

Talukdar, S. 2017. "Indian Soldiers Beheaded on LoC: Time for Hard Decisions but Narendra

Modi Must First Set His House in Order." FirstPost, May 2. Accessed 15 July 2018. https://

www.firstpost.com/india/indian-soldiers-beheaded-on-loc-time-for-hard-decisions-butnarendra-modi-must-first-set-his-house-in-order-3419068.html

Tankel, S. 2011. Storming the World Stage: The Story of Lashkar-E-Taiba. Gurgaon, India:Hachette India.

Tellis, A. 1997. Stability in South Asia. Documented Briefing DB-185-A. Santa Monica, CA:RAND.

Thapar, V. 2008. "'Military Options against Pak Not Easy.'" IBN Live, December 6. Accessed 18

June 2012. http://ibnlive.in.com/news/striking-pak-indias-military-options/79810-3.htmldoi:10.1094/PDIS-11-11-0999-PDN.

Tiwary, D. 2017. "Lashkar-E-Toiba Behind Uri Attack, Says N.I.A." Indian Express, January 31. Accessed 26 March 2018. http://indianexpress.com/article/india/lashkar-e-toiba-behind-uriattack-says-nia-4482725/

Index

About the Author

Musa Khan Jalalzai is a journalist and research scholar. He has written extensively on Afghanistan, terrorism, nuclear and biological terrorism, human trafficking, drug trafficking, and intelligence research and analysis. He was an Executive Editor of the Daily Outlook Afghanistan from 2005-2011, and a permanent contributor in Pakistan's daily *The Post*, *Daily Times*, and *The Nation*, *Weekly the Nation*, (London). However, in 2004, US Library of Congress in its report for South Asia mentioned him as the biggest and prolific writer. He received Masters in English literature, Diploma in Geospatial Intelligence, University of Maryland, Washington DC, certificate in Surveillance Law from the University of Stanford, USA, and diploma in Counter terrorism from Pennsylvania State University, California, the United States.